A STROKE OF MIDNIGHT...

Out of the darkness, back to Light!

John L. Stump

Dr. John L. Stump

Alternative Concepts Publishing House
P.O. Box 1390
Fairhope, AL 35533

A Stroke of Midnight

Copyright @ 2019 by John L. Stump

All rights reserved under International and
Pan-American Copyright Convention

Without limiting the rights of copyright reserved above, no part of this book maybe reproduced or transmitted in any form or by any means (electrical or mechanical, including photocopying, recording, or by any information storage and retrieval system) without prior written permission of both the copyright owner and the above publisher of this book.

Library of Congress Control Number:
ISBN 9781945190308

FV-10HB
Manufactured in the United States of America

First Edition 2007

Author contact: Doc@DocStump.com

A STROKE OF MIDNIGHT...

To Dianne: my guardian angel.

You took care of me during my time of need.

You had the courage of a solider.

The compassion of Mother Teresa,

You were teacher, protector and chauffer.

You live the love we promised each other.

Dr. John L. Stump

A STROKE OF MIDNIGHT...

Preface

This book provides an account of the progress I have made over the five years since I experienced my stroke and was written to help those who suffer a stroke and, more importantly, to help others prevent a stroke. The book is not a textbook but simply the story of my struggle back from near death. It is not my intent to contribute to the advancement of medical knowledge but merely to recount the experience faced when a stroke occurs. My goal has been to create a book to educate and inform people about stroke survival.

Even today many people think of strokes as somehow related to heart attacks. They are more accurately thought of as *brain attacks,* as described by Dr. Vladimir Hachinski in his book *Stroke.* A stroke is a disruption of the blood supply to the brain, either from outside or from inside the brain. When the blood supply is cut to part of the brain, it does not receive the needed oxygen, resulting in damaged tissues and cells of the brain. The common medical term for a stroke is a cerebrovascular accident (CVA).

A stroke influences not only one's body and mind but also one's relationships with others and more importantly…oneself! This is the story of my journey after a sudden stroke in 1999. It took me five years to get to the stage where I could write about what actually happened to me during that time, and ten more years of application.

What I hope to accomplish with this book is to describe events from the day before my stroke to where I am today, as a stroke survivor. And the trials and tribulations I went through, which millions just like me are confronted with each and every day. As a stroke survivor, I want people to understand now I have even more appreciation and acknowledgement for life, and how important it is to let others know you love and care for them and live life to the fullest before being faced with mortality.

It is my wish to help educate the public about the signs and symptoms of cardiovascular disease and stroke, and to present a view of preventive and integrative medicine that may be used by everyone to help prevent a stroke. You may not know that while typing this manuscript **Stroke** moved into second place for cause of death in the world and is projected to become the leading cause of death by the year 2030, these statistics were released by the **American Stroke Association** and the **World Stroke Association** on **World Stroke Day**, October 26, 2013.

If you find the information in this book helpful, please share it with others! I invite you to write me at the address below or contact me by email for further information on stroke survival if you feel the need. I also invite you to help in building a new healthcare system that will recognize the benefits of integrative and alternative healthcare methods to help prevent strokes from occurring in the first place.

John L. Stump, DC, PhD, EdD
365 Section Street
Fairhope, Alabama 36532
Doc@DocStump.com

Foreword

My friend Harvey played tennis every day and golfed twice weekly. He consumed what he thought were healthful foods and practiced moderation in all things. Even into his seventies he appeared to be in peak condition. Then Harvey suffered a stroke. I stopped by to visit and he met me with a smothering hug and lopsided grin. Harvey was always interested in my writing, so I launched into a description of the novel-in-progress. His response floored me.

Although the sounds he made had the flow and rhythm of language, not a word made sense. I was listening to an alien tongue.

It was shocking and distressing. My intelligent, articulate friend babbled incoherently. Flustered and distressed, I treated him like a toddler whose nonsensical vocabulary is not yet coherent.

Dear God, I wish I'd had this book to read.

A Stroke of Midnight should be required reading for anyone who is affected by a cerebrovascular accident, and that includes "victims" who know them and care for them. In this book we learn what the afflicted patient is suffering, and thinking. Dr. John L. Stump is uniquely qualified to teach us about the road to recovery following a stroke, because he has endured it.

Anyone can be felled by a similar calamity. Overnight, careers can crash; personal relations are altered, sometimes permanently. Dr. Stump's life changed in a few devastating moments.

DR. JOHN L. STUMP

This book should scare the hell out of the reader, and at the same time offer a practical assessment of the possibility of regaining normal life after a stroke.

Dr. Stump's *A Stroke Of Midnight* could save your life!

C. Terry Cline, Jr.
Author

A STROKE OF MIDNIGHT...

**Dianne & John Stump at 2006 Rotary Awards banquet
Fairhope, Alabama**

DR. JOHN L. STUMP

Acknowledgments

No book is an accomplishment of the author alone and this one is certainly no exception. I want to thank the many people who helped me get over the hurdles stroke victims face and allowed me to make a new life; everyone from the EMT to the hospital personnel had a hand in helping me over the hurdles. Just their kindness and their smiles were sometimes enough to get me to the next day.

I want to give a special thanks to Christine Linson for the beautiful book cover artwork. This was a perfect picture depicting the downtown clock in the city of Fairhope about to strike midnight done by Christine and adapted to the book at her direction.

I want to also thank Rick Pezikian for his talented hand for doing the pen and ink illustrations of the human body these illustrations were drawn by a man who knows and understands the emphasis of this book.

I also want to thank my friends, colleagues, and the many professionals who answered the thousand questions I asked while working on this book. I know the editing was a challenge but Suzanne Barnhill got me off to a good start. Nancy E. Lynch corrected my West Virginia influenced grammar. Kaa Byington of New York fame gave me an independent edit. But it was the eminent author Terry Cline who really put an eagle eye on the manuscript and had several helpful editing tips.

My scholarly and talented daughter Mariah did the final medical editing for which I am most grateful. But most of all, I want to thank my wonderful wife for being my most unrelenting supporter and number one editor who was there for my every need throughout this whole ordeal...thank you again, Dianne, from the bottom of my heart.

JLS

Table of Contents

Chapter 1	What Happened?	Page 9
Chapter 2	What Was I Experiencing?	Page 26
Chapter 3	Mercy…Not For Me	Page 31
Chapter 4	Therapy, Therapy, Therapy	Page 37
Chapter 5	Climb Back Up The Hill	Page 47
Chapter 6	Another Mountain	Page 68
Chapter 7	New Era	Page 72
Chapter 8	Lame Dancer	Page 76
Chapter 9	Return To Teaching	Page 80
Chapter 10	Personal Therapy	Page 84
Chapter 11	To Sell or Not To Sell	Page 88
Chapter 12	A New Millennium	Page 92
Chapter 13	Back On The Road Again	Page 98
Chapter 14	Getting Back On The Horse	Page 103
Chapter 15	Family, Friends & Others	Page 110
Chapter 16	My Caregiver's View	Page 117
Chapter 17	Preventive Medicine	Page 125
Chapter 18	Tying It All Together	Page 140

DR. JOHN L. STUMP

A STROKE OF MIDNIGHT...

Out of the darkness, back to Light!

DR. JOHN L. STUMP

Chapter 1

What Happened?

*I have worried about many things in my life…
most of which didn't happen.*
Author unknown

I had just returned from Richmond, Virginia, in May 1999 where I had presented an informative program on acupuncture for the International Academy of Medical Acupuncture (IAMA). Organized in 1975, the IAMA is an international organization that teaches and spreads the benefits of acupuncture worldwide but especially to American doctors. I had been teaching with the IAMA for four years. The flight back to Mobile, Alabama had been uneventful. I had used the four or so hours of travel time to plan an upcoming lecture. After treating patients next week in my Sports Medicine practice, I was to be off for the next month on a working vacation to New Zealand.

I felt now would be a good time for Dianne and me to take a nice long trip. Chad, our oldest, was through the University of Delaware, and Mike, the middle sibling, had finished the University of Tennessee and was in graduate school in San Francisco. Mariah, our youngest, was now through Washington College in Maryland, and wrestling with whether to go straight to medical school or go to graduate school for her master's degree before going on to medical school. Dianne and I both felt we had accomplished a feat with our children graduating from college and that we both deserved a break. Additionally, the trip could be a tax write-off for presenting a portion of the research accumulated during the Seoul Olympics at the combined conference of the New Zealand Sports Medicine Association, World Sports Federation, and the World Federation of Chiropractic.

I got home from the Richmond acupuncture lecture about 5:00 P.M. on a delightful Sunday evening. This was going to be the week Dianne and I spent getting ready to go to New Zealand. However, tonight we were going out to celebrate. We figured we would go to LuLu's Lounge, owned and operated by my patient Lucy Buffett, Jimmy Buffett's sister. The restaurant was on Weeks Bay just off Mobile Bay and the Gulf of Mexico. The restaurant was only minutes from our house, and offered wonderful fresh seafood.

We ordered our usual, grouper sandwiches with fried green tomatoes and cheese. We stayed and listened to the music until about 10:00 P.M., then headed back home because we wanted to do some more packing for the trip.

Arriving home, we got most of the packing out of the way, and then, while getting ready for bed, we got in that lovin' mood and decided to end the week right! When I got up from the bed, I noticed I had a very heavy feeling in my right arm and then my right leg. I fell back on the bed because I could not stand. I tried to explain to Dianne the feeling I was experiencing. I had no pain, but I knew something was wrong. Dianne asked me to call someone. I started again to get up and then to speak and could not. I tried to move my arm again and could not. I fell back onto the bed. With fear in her eyes, Dianne immediately called 911.

Then she called Mike and Sue Moore, our neighbors, who lived only a few houses down the bay from us. Mike said he would be right down. Dianne rushed to get dressed and then to dress me. By that time, about ten minutes had passed. I noticed I had no feeling in my right arm or right leg and, although I could move my mouth, only animal sounds would come out. Nothing could be articulated—believe me I tried.

Our neighbor arrived; he and Dianne were telling me to take it easy and things would be better when the emergency personnel arrived. During this time I tried to tell them I was having no pain and thought I would be fine. Even when I thought of stroke symptoms I denied the possibility I was having a stroke because I had no symptoms! Lying there on the bed I looked up at the clock. There was 10 minutes before the stroke of midnight by our clock.

Soon thereafter the emergency personnel arrived. The two EMTs were small in stature, so they had a little trouble getting my 200 pounds on the stretcher, and then because our beach house was built up on pilings to avoid possible flooding, there was some discussion about who was going down the steps first. It was about that time that I seemed to go to sleep; actually I slipped into a coma, much like a sleep. I seemed to have conscious episodes a few minutes at a time until in the hospital. About the last thing I remember was lying on a gurney being wheeled down a hall with several doctors and nurses hovering above me and seeing a clock that read midnight. Now I know I was in Thomas Hospital's emergency room in Fairhope, Alabama.

For those unfamiliar with stroke damage to the brain, this account of my stroke may seem disjointed. It is intended to be. After coming out of the coma I did not or could not process much of anything for many months. What I am giving you are the bits and pieces I got until I could process everything neurologically, which was months if not years, Dianne tells me.

At first it was like I was in some type of time warp. I could see and hear people; they were smiling at me and talking to me as if I understood...but I did not! I didn't even know where I was or what was happening to me. I was in a strange new world all alone not knowing anyone, it seemed. People would be right in my face where I could not miss them or what they said, but it was like pouring water in a sieve; nothing wanted to stay. I really couldn't see very well either for some reason; later I would find that it was because I was left with double vision for six weeks after the stroke.

I seemed to wake from a deep sleep, for I remember dreaming a lot during that period, but I will have to dig a little deeper into my subconscious for those memories. I first saw Dianne but did not know her name and was not sure who she was. I tried to speak, and no words would come out, only sounds. Dianne smiled and said for me not to try so hard yet, that I was at the hospital and had suffered a massive stroke. I had been in a coma, unconscious, for nearly three weeks. This was my first acknowledgment of anything during those weeks, she told me. "Your blood pressure is still not stabilized, and the right side of your body as well as your speech was affected," Dianne said. All of this was Greek to me. I was not sure what she said and was really concerned about not being able to see normally. Of course I didn't know that the double vision was not normal until Dianne asked the doctor why I kept rubbing my eyes. I tried to tell her about my vision but couldn't; it was as if we spoke two different languages.

This was strange. I had been in excellent health all my life, although there were some injuries I could remember—like the time I was showing off for a girl and tried to dive from a high dive through an inner tube about twelve feet below. I was knocked out when my head didn't make it through the tube as fast as my body. My body didn't surface as it should have, and several of the boys I was with had to pull me out and revive me. Also, there was the time I was shot out of a tree stealing oranges in Palm Bay, Florida, where we lived at the time (I was about twelve or thirteen). I was walking home from a dance at the teen center, and the moonlight was shining on these beautiful oranges, and I just had to have one. Later the owner said he yelled for the trespasser to get out, but I ignored him, and he shot a warning shot up into the air… that happened to hit me in the back!

Then there was the broken neck I sustained my first year of college. That injury ended my up-and-coming football career. Then later, when I was coaching, there was a bad traffic accident when a big-rig truck ran the school bus off the road. This was a small school, so we coaches had to drive the bus sometimes, and this night I was bringing the players and cheerleaders back to John Carroll High School in Fort Pierce, Florida. The road from Okeechobee was a small two-lane road, and it was late. On each side of the road were large drainage ditches with no shoulder to pull over when someone was in such a hurry to pass. The truck went by and cut back in front of us too closely, causing me to swerve off the road and the bus to slide into the drainage ditch.

That accident introduced me to chiropractic. The doctors at the hospital had wanted to do surgery on me because the injury had herniated a lumbar disc in my back. Surgery, they said, was the only thing that could help. I remembered what Dr. Mendoza (my orthopaedist) had told me when I sustained the broken neck: not to have surgery unless there was no other choice. That's what I decided to do. I told another General Practitioner there in Fort Pierce who was on the board at the high school, and he agreed that I should not have surgery without at least a second or third opinion.

In short, I ended up going to a chiropractor that had me walking without pain in a little over six weeks. By that time school was about over for the year, and I was told not to do anything physical for the next four or five weeks. I was a coach and the athletic director; everything I did was physical; so school officials told me to take the remainder of the year off.

I told the chiropractor about my situation, and he suggested I consider going back to school. After all, I had my master's degree, so it wouldn't take long to get a doctorate. I went home, talked to my wife, and later decided to give up coaching and to return to the classroom.

Then there was this broken leg in a boating accident trying to teach our son, Mike, to use the hand-held rudder of a skiff we had while living on Mobile Bay. Mike had gotten accelerating and decelerating mixed up as we approached a pier. We ended up crashing against the pier, and in an effort to prevent any more collateral damage I had jumped in the stern to shut the engine off and ended up breaking the fibula in my right lower leg.

I'd also broken toes in Shorinji Kempo when I was taking my second-*dan* black belt test at the very prestigious Kongo Zen Doin (Temple) of Sensei Yamamori in Los Angeles. During the sparring portion of the test, I kicked at the *doi* (chest protector) of my opponent, Kuramoto sensei, and caught my toes somehow on the edge of the protector. You could hear the crack all over the dojo, but I did not stop. I had spent several years preparing for this test so, a few broken toes were not going to keep me from finishing the test even though the pain was terrible. My toe next to the big toe is a little longer than the big toe. Somehow when I had kicked that toe was the one that had made contact with the chest protector. Now, it was sticking out the opposite direction from the other toes on that foot because, I had not pulled back my toes to the degree I should have!

Also, there was the time I went out on the pier one cold fall morning to see if the bay had frozen. I was wearing cowboy boots because I was leaving for Mexico the next day, and I wanted to be sure the boots felt comfortable. It was still dark, and I could not tell that our pipes had frozen and burst, and there was ice all over the pier. I went skating right toward the water; in a great effort not to go over into the cold surf, I somehow threw myself into the unyielding rail very, very hard. I ended up with a cracked tibia in my left leg that I had my assistant set after we X-rayed it that morning in my office. I was determined not to let that alter my plans for a trip to Mexico; I'd had the tickets for a month, and all the guys had been talking for weeks about all the plans for the annual trip to the hunting and fishing lodge.

As you can see, I had sustained some major injuries but being chronically ill had not been part of my life. I was always happy and healthy—not so much as even a headache. But was this stroke an injury or an illness or both?

Suddenly I was brought back from my mental wondering by a nurse who came in to check on me. It seems they had been keeping a pretty close watch on me because of my blood pressure problems. I could not understand how I could remember all those old times and injuries, yet have no idea of recent events or basic data such as my wife's name (or anyone else's for that matter). Where was I and what had happened and why I couldn't I see, talk, or walk?

I would later find out that massive strokes like mine had the result of wiping out the short-term memory and allowing the long-term memory to survive. This occurs when a lesion of the brain occurs in a particular area. The bleeding of the brain in this particular area allowed the blood to pool and cause damage to the surrounding tissues. I can now understand why a stroke used to be called ***apoplexy***, from a Greek word meaning '*to strike down.*' Unlike the painful symptoms of a heart attack, the warnings of a stroke can be subtle and the effects more lasting. Basic functions like walking, talking, thinking, and sight as well as personality may be changed temporarily or permanently in a number of cases. I know I certainly felt "struck down' or was it knocked down, as I lay in the hospital bed.

The function that is lost when a particular part of the brain is damaged gives us clues to where the stroke occurred and how much impairment may be expected. The brain seems capable of remarkable recuperation if it can convalesce from damage like mine.

The human brain is incredibly complex as I thought back on my neuroanatomy classes at Palmer College of Chiropractic in Davenport, Iowa with Dr. Schmeidel. It's made up of billions of nerve cells called neurons, each communicating with thousands of others, allowing us to think, move, and live our amazing lives. For the human brain to function at peak levels, blood must flow through all of its many vessels. If blood flow is obstructed in any way, the blocked part of the brain loses its energy supply and becomes injured. Obstruction for more than a few minutes results in permanent brain tissue injury and death of the affected region. The loss or alteration of bodily function that results from an insufficient supply of blood to a part of the brain is what I had experienced.

Stroke is the third leading cause of death in the United States, after diseases of the heart and forms of cancer. About 600,000 Americans have strokes each year, about one person every 53 seconds. Stroke occurs suddenly and is the leading cause of serious, longstanding disability, accounting for more than half of all the hospitalizations for neurological diseases.

About 4.5 million stroke survivors live today and 2.2 million of them are male; you can see there is not much difference in male and female stroke incidence. Stroke is estimated to cost $30–$40 billion each year in the United States alone.

As we continue my story I will try to give you enough medical detail to be accurate without boring you.

More tests were to follow to try to unravel the mystery of my stroke event. Why did a stroke strike me down, a healthy person with no apparent outward symptoms? Before I tell of how and why this happened at this time in my life, let me give you a few facts about stroke.

What is a Stroke?

Stroke is caused by a lack of blood supply to a portion of the brain, which causes that area to die within minutes. This lack of blood supply, also known as ischemia, results in long-term neurological effects because the cells in the brain are directly affected. Although stroke is associated with older people it can occur at any age. As Americans we have a much higher incidence of stroke than those in other countries.

The diminished blood supply to the brain that occurs during a stroke may be the result of several factors:
- Atherosclerosis (fatty deposits) of the arteries to the brain and neck
- Blood clots that close off these arteries
- A mobile clot (embolus) that lodges in an artery that supplies the brain with blood
- Cerebral hemorrhage

If we consider an isolated blood vessel, blood flow to brain tissue can be hampered in two ways.
- In an *ischemic stroke*, the blood vessel clogs within

- In a ***hemorrhagic stroke,*** the blood vessel ruptures, causing the blood to leak into the brain. (This was my type.)

Ischemic stroke accounts for more than 80% of all stroke cases. It results from obstruction of a blood vessel, typically a blood clot. Such a clot is called a ***cerebral thrombus*** or a ***cerebral embolism.*** Atherosclerosis is an underlying condition for this type of obstruction. The fatty deposits of atherosclerosis can cause two types of obstruction.

- *Cerebral thrombosis* refers to a thrombus that develops at the clogged part of the vessel.
- *Cerebral embolism* refers generally to a blood clot that forms at another location in the circulatory system, usually the heart and large arteries of the upper chest and neck. A portion of this blood clot breaks loose, enters the bloodstream, and travels through the brain's blood vessels until it reaches a vessel too small to let it pass, creating a blockage.

Hemorrhagic stroke such as mine occurs when a weakened blood vessel ruptures and bleeds into the surrounding brain tissue, compromising it and causing damage. Two types of weakened blood vessels usually cause hemorrhagic stroke.

- An *aneurysm* is a ballooning of the tissue of a weakened region of a blood vessel. If left untreated, the aneurysm continues to weaken until it ruptures and bleeds into the brain.
- An *arteriovenous malformation* (AVM) is a cluster of abnormally formed blood vessels. Any one of these vessels can rupture, also causing bleeding into the brain.

Stroke prevention is improved by decreasing atherosclerosis. Reduction of atherosclerosis and thrombosis risk is the primary therapeutic goal once a stroke such as mine has occurred.

Dr. John L. Stump

Warning Signs of Stroke

If you notice one or more of these signs in yourself or another person, don't wait: call 911 or your local emergency medical services number immediately. Studies show that you are better off if you get to the hospital right away; treatment is more effective if administered quickly. Every second counts!

Although most people who suffer strokes are older, stroke can occur at any age. Especially prone are people with unhealthy lifestyles—those who smoke, stick to poor dietary habits, and don't exercise. Stroke is also highly associated with people who suffer from obesity, high blood pressure, heart disease, diabetes and alcohol abuse, or have a family history of stroke or abnormal heart rhythm. In the United States, statistics show that African-Americans have a much higher incidence of stroke.

The signs are:
- Sudden numbness or weakness in the face, arm, or leg, especially on one side of the body
- Sudden confusion, trouble speaking or understanding
- Sudden trouble seeing in one or both eyes
- Sudden trouble walking, dizziness, loss of balance or coordination
- Sudden, severe headache with no known cause

Not all of these signs occur with every stroke. Sometimes they go away and return. If some occur, get help as soon as possible.

It has been shown if you lose weight, your cholesterol, blood pressure and diabetes will improve. These are all called risk factors. Losing weight single-handedly knocks out three of the big risk factors. No one likes to talk about it, but honestly, losing weight is the key to whittling down the risk factors to a minimum.

Two medical tests are sometimes used to help prevent stroke if a person has two or three risk factors. Carotid artery disease is an independent risk factor for stroke. A carotid ultrasound is used to detect blockages or fatty buildup in the carotid arteries on either side of the neck. A physician must evaluate a patient's overall risk factors to determine if the patient is a candidate for ultrasound. Those with vascular disease, hypertension, high cholesterol, smoker or are elderly are going to be most at risk and should be screened with additional tests. My father, a former coalminer in West Virginia, died as the result of black lung disease and he was a smoker until just a few years before his death. But, even at the late age of 76 he felt better and the doctor said he would have gained a few more years of life if he had decided to quit a little sooner. A person who decides to stop smoking benefits almost immediately.

At 20 minutes after quitting:
- Blood pressure decreases
- Pulse rate drops
- Body temperature of hands and feet increases

At 8 hours:
- Carbon monoxide level in blood drops to normal
- Oxygen level in blood returns to normal

At 24 hours:
- Chance of heart attack decreases

At 48 hours:
- Nerve endings in the lungs will start to re-grow
- Ability to smell and taste improves

As you can see the progress continues for each day that one remains "smoke free." We could continue to list the benefits of not smoking but let's get back to the subject.

The ankle brachial index is the second medical test. This is a simple non-invasive test that can be performed in a physician's office when there is cardiovascular compromise indicated. The ankle brachial index (ABI) compares blood pressures in the arms to blood pressures in the legs and can indicate if a patient has peripheral artery disease or plaque buildup in the body's arteries.

The ABI is a good way to screen for stroke or categorize people in a cardiovascular group of either high or low risk. Neither the carotid ultrasound nor the ABI test will detect strokes caused by small vessel intracranial (vessels within the brain) diseases that account for about half of the strokes that occur.

Paying close attention to risk factors is the best defense against stroke. As we venture ahead we will discuss more about risk factors and how they can be improved.

What is a TIA (transient ischemic attack)?

My mother-in-law, Myrtle Bearden, whom I dearly love, is 87 and subject to the phenomenon described as a ***transient ischemic attack*** (TIA). She has noticed this problem for the past ten years. She has been to several doctors numerous times, and they can find nothing that brings this on. She cannot be prescribed any medication that can prevent these TIAs from occurring. The doctors tell her they will keep an eye on her. What does that mean—wait until something happens to put her in the hospital?

A TIA is a "mini-stroke" or "pre-stroke" with the same signs as a stroke, but the signs only last a few minutes. This is a short-term lack of blood supply to the brain. This condition is often a precursor to a full-scale stroke, so any symptoms associated with it should be investigated immediately. The loss of blood supply last from seconds to minutes and does not result in permanent damage.

About 10% of strokes are preceded by TIAs. In the United States alone, physicians have diagnosed TIA in about 4.9 million Americans. Experts say just as many or more have had a TIA that went unrecognized and untreated. TIA has no traditional medical treatment other than a suggestion of daily aspirin. However, in people who have had one or more TIAs, about 36% will eventually have a stroke. A person who has had more than one, like Myrtle, is 9.5 times more at risk for a stroke.

Many conditions can masquerade as a TIA including, but not limited to, migraine headaches, seizures, and low blood sugar or brain tumor. Symptoms usually last less than a day, so it's easy to think that the problem has gone away. They cause no lasting damage because the disruption of blood to the brain is brief. Research has shown in recent studies that risk of having a stroke within days or a few weeks of a TIA are considerably higher than the previously suspected 1 or 2 percent chance. Research published in a 2003 journal of *Stroke* showed that people who have had a TIA have a nine percent chance of having a stroke within a week, and a 12 percent chance within a month.

TIAs are extremely important stroke warning signs. Don't ignore them. This is where preventative medicine plays a vital role in stroke prevention. By decreasing atherosclerosis and other health risk factors, the possibility of stroke is reduced. Studies have shown that the omega-3 fatty acid *eicosapantaenoic acid* (EPA) is a helpful factor in reducing platelet aggregation and thrombosis. There are many other preventative factors that are important that we will cover in a later chapter.

The outcome of stroke depends on the person's age, general health, the region of the brain affected, the type of stroke, and the extent of brain damage. This is the story of my recovery from this stealth attack on my health. Let's proceed with my story as it happened a few years ago. I will be giving you stroke facts and figures as we proceed with the story.

As I lay there in the hospital bed I really couldn't think of anything other than random thought processes that seem to be like flashes of light going off in my head. I had tubes going into every body cavity. I knew something terrible happened but at that time I wasn't sure what. People asked me do you hurt? How could you not hurt with all that was happening? But, I couldn't talk, I couldn't even see because of a vision problem the doctor said comes with a stroke sometimes.

What was my prognosis? At this point, Dianne tells me, the doctors didn't want to give a prognosis. They were not certain of the diagnosis that had caused the stroke. On the following pages you will find some drawings of the brain and the illustrations depicting the areas of the brain of my stroke.

Human brain

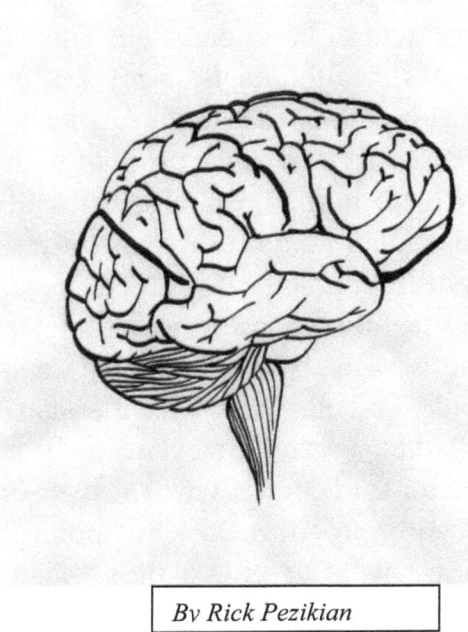

By Rick Pezikian

Illustration 1. Side view of the human brain

A STROKE OF MIDNIGHT...

THE HUMAN BRAIN

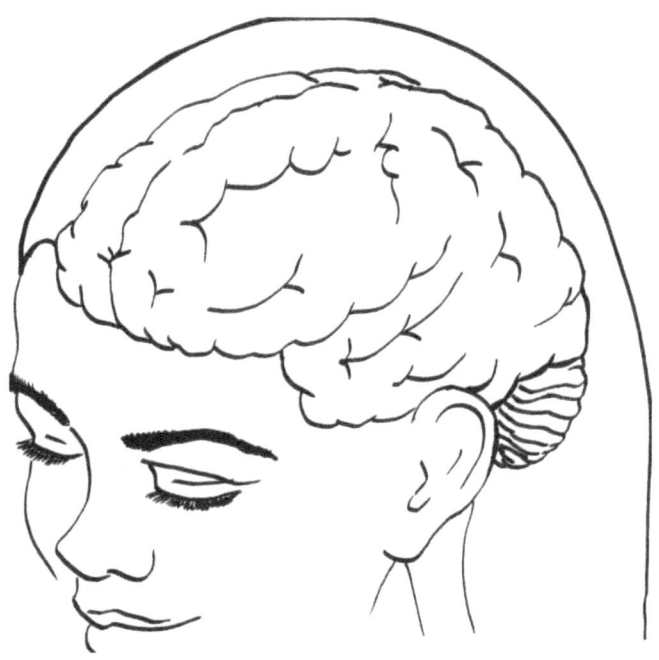

Illustration 2. Brain inside the human head

By Rick Pezikian

STRUCTURES OF THE BRAIN

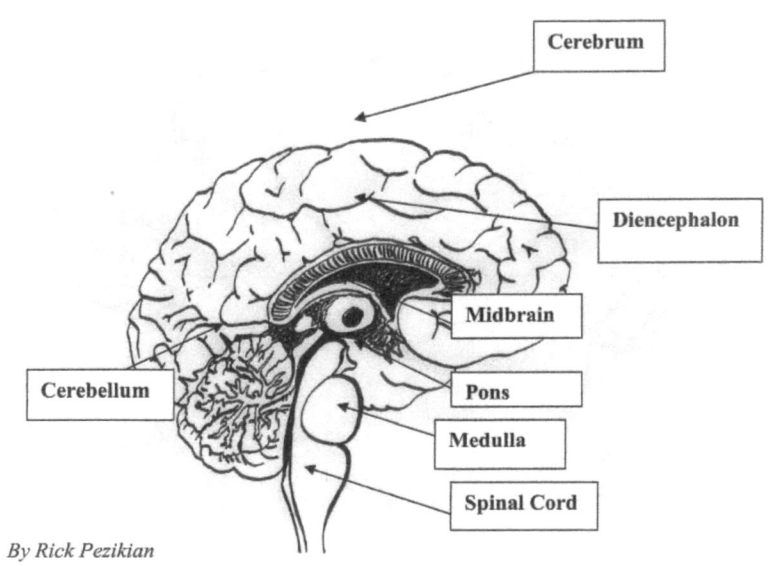

Illustration 3. Structures of the human brain

A STROKE OF MIDNIGHT...

THE BRAIN CONTROLS THE BODY

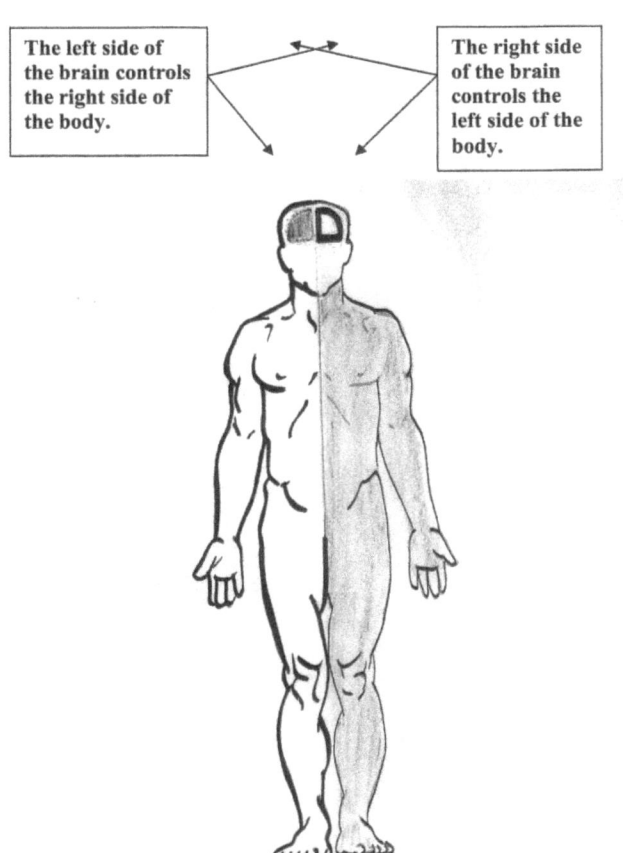

By Rick Pezikian

DR. JOHN L. STUMP

Stump wheelchair bound after stroke
"401 Professional Centre" wins award ES Chamber of Commerce - 1999

Doc gets help walking after "stroke."
Mercy Medical Hospital
Daphne, AL

Dr. Stump at the Rehabilitation Hospital after his stroke

Chapter 2

What Was I Experiencing?

The way we look at life determines our experience.
Author unknown

We all try to find meaning in new experiences in our lives, in the hope that we can learn something about how we should lead our lives in the future as well as how to handle the present. That was certainly the case for me now. The story of the beginning and progress of my experience is critical for it serves to preserve the history of the incident and remind us constantly that it occurred as quickly and stealthily as a thief in the night.

As I faded in and out of reality, I could see our children, and that made me happy. Whether or not I was able to communicate with them at that time was not the point. I hope they knew from my smile that I was glad to see them. That Chad had taken time from his new job to come down and be with me was wonderful. He had graduated from the University of Delaware and taken a job at Allen Family Foods on the Delmarva Peninsula. He was in a new management-training program the poultry business was developing. I knew he had been trying to communicate with me and I with him, but the words were just not there. I knew that I should understand him and what he was trying to communicate to me, but I did not.

There was Mike, who was having a problem with the University of Tennessee at Knoxville. The computers had crashed and caused a lot of problems with finding the courses he had taken and he was starting graduate school in San Francisco. I could hear him talking to me, and I think I tried to say a few words but could not manage what I wanted to say. I had wanted to explain that the courses were important, but they were electives, and would be found by the computer department if he would just be patient. Mike had graduated an English major after the geology major did not work out for him. Now he was going on to graduate school until he could decide what he wanted to pursue for a career.

Then there was Mariah, who was much like her poppa in every way. She was in her last year at Washington College in Chestertown, Maryland. She had a few grades of A– in Organic Chemistry and in Physics but still maintained a 3.9 GPA. The grades were not the problem; it was the decision of whether to go straight into medical school or go to graduate school first. We had discussed it several times, but she was still not sure what she wanted to do with her life at that point. I had tried to tell her to relax for several months while she thought about it after graduation. This she was still wrestling with and was trying to explain her plans to me. I really wanted her to go on to graduate school instead of medical school since she was so young. She had graduated a year ahead of her regular high school class. She was very academic but had trouble making decisions. But the decisions she finally came up with were usually correct ones. Whereas I was a quick decision maker and had often regretted a particular decision so it meant that I had to take the long road to get to a particular point, Mariah may take longer but never had to backtrack or regret a decision. Mariah was my girl for sure. She even looked like me tall, blonde hair and blue eyes and always smiling, people would say.

Lying in bed was certainly not helping any of the kids. I had tubes coming out of every orifice—two and three out of some. I couldn't move and my mind was focused only for brief periods of time. Even when it was focused, I could not talk. I did not know when, where, or how things were happening, or any of the things that Dianne or the doctors asked. I thought about my martial arts training. I would need the self-discipline now for sure.

Then the nurses cleared everyone from the room. It was time to make another change, I suppose. What was it this time I wondered? There was a lot of talk and discussion between the doctor and the head nurse. Another tube was to come out of me... I overheard them say. Which body part would they choose this time? Of about five people that I recognized from being there before, Dianne was the only one allowed in the room. The nursing and hospital staff was all matter-of-fact, not unkind, but very impersonal. They had a job to do, and they were going to get it done. I recognized this from being in a health care profession for so many years.

Later, I found out I was in Thomas Hospital in Fairhope, Alabama, for several weeks. The Thomas hospital and the ER staff had saved my life, it seems. After nearly three weeks of critical care they had my blood pressure somewhat stabilized, as best they could, and decided to move me to Mercy Medical Hospital in Daphne, Alabama. Today, I only remember bits and pieces of the time before my stay at Mercy Medical, even though many have said they came by for a minute or two to visit me. It is as if this period was a dream...or should I say a nightmare? I remember having some strange dreams, but I am not prepared to elaborate on them at this time. I'm still not sure what was accurate and what was a dream state at that time.

The daily struggle was now setting in. I remembered that yesterday was in the past and tomorrow is in the future. The fragmented pieces of my life were coming back a little each day. When Dianne said that a lot of my patients were asking about how I was doing, I remembered that I was a doctor. Now another piece of the puzzle was coming together. I thought for a while, and then the doctor part of the story came back to me. When this stroke happened, I had been a chiropractor and acupuncturist, as well as a traveling lecturer on Oriental Medicine. I had been in practice over 25 years and loved every minute of the professional challenges. Now my stroke was the biggest test of my life. The many challenges I had experienced throughout the years did not compare to this one, not even my broken neck!

I remember we were planning a lecture tour to New Zealand when this happened. It looked like we had missed that trip! The planned New Zealand adventure had come about as a result of a series of events that had really started happening nearly 25 years earlier, when I did my Sports Medicine Internship at the Peninsula General Hospital in Salisbury, Maryland.

As a chiropractor, I had become intrigued with acupuncture theory and philosophy; I had been fascinated with the five thousand year old history of acupuncture and how it had worked so well for the millions of patients for so long, without being acknowledged by western science. In 1972, I had seen its effectiveness demonstrated a number of times by Dr. Shingo Fukinbara, a fellow student at Chiropractic College, who later became my *sensei* (teacher) and mentor in both acupuncture and the martial art of Shorinji Kempo. The ancient fighting art of Shorinji Kempo had captured my interest as much as acupuncture because I was already a black belt in Karate and Judo.

As a result of this interest in acupuncture and martial arts, upon my graduation from chiropractic school, I went to Japan, for a three-year post-doctoral program in acupuncture. You might say the Orient captivated me. I went on to study from several masters in Japan, China, India, and Tibet, even walking through south China with groups of monks that *sensei* had told me how to get in touch with when I got to the Chinese mainland. I reflected that Fukinbara sensei had wanted my acupuncture education to be more than just a classroom didactic experience...it certainly was that.

Dr. Fukinbara started my interest in sports medicine from an eastern perspective about that time. For my scope had been only western medicine up to that point in my career. However, Professor Fukinbara expanded my horizon considerably when I opened the door to Acupuncture and Oriental Medicine, to which he introduced me.

In 1985, I was invited to go to South Korea to become a team doctor for the Sang Mu (Military) Team, in order for them to get ready for the 1986 Asian Games and the 1988 Olympics. I guess my acupuncture background and the years spent in the Orient had caught the Sport Medicine Officials attention.

I could not stay in Korea, as the Olympic Committee had wanted, but instead I struck a deal of going over for a week or so once a month, and even this became very difficult, with fifteen trips to Seoul before the '86 Asian Games and the '88 Olympic Games hadn't even started! The South Korean team was ready, but I was worn out, because during this two-year period of time I was also beginning to work with the United States Sports Academy in Daphne, Alabama, on sports projects but I was still living in Delmar, Delaware.

The chiropractic work I was doing with the South Korean team had led to the deepened acupuncture interest by the South Korean Olympic Committee. They wanted me to do acupuncture for their athletes when they needed it utilized, as well as, chiropractic. They saw no reason why our International Chiropractor's Sports Committee could not do both. It all had completely absorbed my interest in health care from a new eastern perspective but I was working for the International Chiropractors Association (ICA) that did not condone acupuncture at that time (1980's). I was in a quandary...what was I going to do?

The Seoul Olympic Committee had organized a scientific group of sports physicians and had called for original research papers to be presented at the conference in Seoul at Dankook University. The International Chiropractors Association and the World Chiropractic Sports Federation was anxious to have the data we had collected from the study with the Olympic athletes presented for the whole scientific sports world to view. I had decided after some urging from Professor Chung Ha Suh, our academic advisor from the University of Colorado, to take the material we had gathered and tie it into my postdoctoral dissertation for Sports Medicine that I had started at the United States Sports Academy.

I was now experiencing the aftermath of the CVA; suddenly and without warning my life was forever changed. In an instant that Sunday night, a blood vessel in my brain had burst, and part of my brain had quit working. I didn't have any warning, not a sign or symptom. Now, I understood why they call this the silent killer! Together, strokes and heart attacks account for nearly three-fourths of all deaths in North America. Was I glad that I was not one of those in that statistic! In the United States, someone experiences a stroke every 53 seconds, and now I was among the four million Americans living with the effects of a stroke.

Out of four people that have a stroke, one will recover fully, one will recover incompletely, one will remain disabled and require assistance the rest of his life, and one will die. After the first stroke, all survivors have a 10% risk, each year, of having another stroke. Where would I fall in this group of stats? Would I be in the 25% that die or in the 25% that fully recovered? I remembered a story in college about Louis Pasteur doing some his best work after suffering a bad stroke. Maybe I would fall into that category, for I did love my work and would hate to not be able to resume at least some phase of it. I knew one thing: I was going to do everything I could to try to be like Pasteur in the stroke recovery category.

Chapter 3

Mercy...Not for Me

The eye sees what it brings to seeing.
Shelly

I had come out of the coma a month before. I had been lying in a hospital bed at Mercy Medical Hospital since that time. Not my longest stay in a hospital, I thought. I had spent three months in the hospital in Easton, Maryland, with a broken neck, under the care of Dr. Alfredo Mendoza, an orthopedist who had advised me not to be operated on, at a time when surgeries were the medical answer for everything. He had also advised me that my football career was over, that when I went back to the University of Maryland it would be as a *former* athlete. He had loaned me book after book to read during my hospital stay. They were his orthopaedic medical texts. Having nothing else to do 24 hours a day, I read them from cover to cover.

I became especially interested in human anatomy. Dr. Mendoza explained what had happened to me and how I was lucky that my spinal cord was not damaged. My muscular neck had saved me from life in a wheelchair, he would say. He even had a pair of prism glasses made for me to read with because I was in a cast from the top of my head to my waist and could not see the books to read except at a certain angle. He told my parents about my passion for reading his medical texts and that I should get these special glasses that would enable me to read more easily while I was immobilized flat on my back.

My parents were a very hard working people from the Appalachian Mountains of West Virginia.

My father, John Flemming Stump, was an astute, hard-working man. Although he only had an eighth-grade formal education, he was very worldly educated. He was one of nine brothers and two sisters and next to the youngest in age. He became a coal miner by trade at the young age of 16. He later became a stone mason and on the weekends and holidays trying to earn enough money to quit the coal mine. He had earned quite a reputation as a musician when he was young. Both he and my mother performed in several bands that played at many of the radio stations and clubs within driving distance from their home and even made several records with a recording studio in Cincinnati, Ohio. He had never quit the coal mine because it was the best-paying job around. He once admitted when we were older, that the danger was quite exciting, giving him an adrenalin rush. He once told me of working for days on his back loading coal in a mineshaft sixteen inches in height. It was about that time that he and another musician by the name of Merle Travis worked on a song about the life of the local miner. Tennessee Ernie Ford later made this song, "Sixteen Tons," famous.

I remember when I was about eleven or twelve and my brother Doug was still in elementary school, my mother sat us down and told us that our father had been seriously hurt in a coal mine accident. Although not expected to live, he pulled through, but he was never able to labor in the coal mine again. We then moved to Aiken, South Carolina where my father began work on a construction crew with E. I. DuPont Company. It seemed like they transferred my father about every three years to another job site all over the country. We had ended up in Delaware, at the corporate headquarters, where my father was building a main building for them from brick and stone. The masonry work got him through the thin times, as mother used to say. She would never say that we were poor but that we were thin on money much of the time.

When Dr. Mendoza told my father the cost of the prism glasses that I needed, he looked at my mother and said, "Well, I guess it's going to be another thin Christmas!" Dr. Mendoza said he would see what he could do. The following week some doctors came in and did some eye tests, and one week later I had a pair of prism glasses to study the textbooks that he would lend me. The staff doctors had gotten together and had arranged for the finances my parents needed to get the glasses.

Now, when I look back on it, I see where I developed my real academic interest in health and the human body. Of course my grandmother also played a significant role, for after I told her of my interest I found out that she had been an herbal healer and midwife in the Appalachian Mountains before marrying my grandfather, who was a railroad engineer on the Norfolk and Western Railroad. While I lay there in the Easton hospital, she had told me of the many herbal remedies used by the Indians and Appalachian country folk. She spent many hours by my bedside explaining herb after herb; she even had sketches she had made of them. I think that my interest in healing gradually grew from those days with Dr. Mendoza and my grandmother.

Now several months after the stroke, my mind was clear enough at times that I could think about my body paralysis. Over the past several weeks the tubes and lifelines had been gradually removed from all the orifices of my body, and I was being sent down two times each day for different exams and to introduce me to the different therapies.

In the past, my health had been nearly perfect. I had not only prided myself on having been an athlete in high school and college but had continued by being involved in marathons, scuba diving, downhill skiing, biking, sky diving, martial arts, hikes, tai chi, qi gong, and long walks and yoga with Dianne. There was not much I didn't like or try. There were a few things like hang-gliding and skydiving that I had tried a few times and not continued because of time or money, but there wasn't much.

I had been teaching Shorinji Kempo, an ancient Zen Buddhist martial art, for over 25 years, and I had used it as a student evaluation system. If they had the motivation and fortitude to finish a black belt in Shorinji Kempo, they were well on their way to a good wholesome life. This I had used for years with the younger students, and now that I was getting more mature, I noticed the same principles held true regardless of age.

In the past, my muscles had always done what they were supposed to do: run, jump, catch, throw, pull, push, twist, one leg or both, eyes open or closed. To become a black belt in Shorinji Kempo required every possible motion, the most difficult and minute muscle functions, and I was the *sensei* (teacher). After all, the students had to even learn to understand and read Japanese *kanji* (characters), which required strokes and motions their hand had never made before...unbelievable, you say! The *kenshi* (student) obtaining the rank of *shodan* (black belt) or above was highly respected in my mind. Even though many good students had started and not quite reached the *Shodan* grade, they had improved their life a great deal just the same. Some were now doctors, lawyers, teachers, engineers, police officers, researchers, and leaders in their respective fields. What was I to do now that I could not be their teacher, their *sensei*?

A person who has never before lost these functions and body movements, even a chiropractor, medical doctor, physical therapist, or any other healthcare professional, cannot understand the full impact of the loss. You like to think that as a doctor you can empathize with your patients. You can read and write about these phenomena and observe another person going through a stroke, but unless you actually experience the trauma and emotion, you can never really know what it is truly like.

After a number of days of lying there just trying to remember events, I thought it was time for a self-assessment. In measuring the stroke damage, I glanced at my flaccid right arm. The appendage seemed lifeless and dead. It didn't seem to be part of me as it had been before. I went on to my right leg; again, there was no movement in it at all. My face was numb on the right side. It seemed the right side of my body was almost perfectly absent. Then I wondered if I had feeling in the right testicle; I would have to check that later! With my entire right side gone, what was my future going to be like? If I wasn't careful here, I could slip into a depressive state, thinking about the past and comparing it to the future. No, this I wouldn't do. Depression and negative behavior had not been a part of my thinking before and were not going to be a part of my thinking now. I had seen too many patients who ended up a slave to their negative thinking, and this had caused them more problems in the long run. I had to look at the big picture no matter what problems I faced.

This was bad, all right, but I had survived much. I had even been struck by lightning a few years back during one of the horrendous thunderstorms that are so prevalent in the South. Now it seemed this was going to be my ultimate challenge. The other incidents had seemed just as traumatic at the time they occurred, but I never let them get me. Why would I buckle under to the effects of this stroke?

I kept going back to the question, why did I have this stroke? I was not overweight, did not smoke, had not experienced dizziness or headache, and I was only 53 years old. I did not have any heart problems, and I had just gone through a physical for the insurance company. Where did this come from? What brought it on? The doctors did not seem to know. Later, as I put the pieces of the puzzle together, I could see where there could have been little signs and symptoms like sweating excessively, always thirsty and less restful sleep, but nothing obvious…like pain or any of the other major signs of stroke. A million things raced through my mind, but nothing seemed to stay. It was as if my mind was a blank at times—actually most of the time. Then I would have spells of lucidity and seemingly perfect clarity. Those times didn't last very long however.

How could I take on so many nearly impossible tasks with only half a body and with my communication skills almost nonexistent? Would my wonderful wife have to attend to me all of the time? I could barely feed myself or go to the toilet, or put my clothes on, let alone go to the hardware store, fix a pump, or trim a branch from a tree! Was I going to be bedridden forever? Would I be confined to a wheelchair for life? Even if I could roll outside, would I ever be able to drive again? Dianne would have to get rid of all my sporting paraphernalia: the Boston Whaler boat, golf clubs, rifles, scuba gear, ski equipment, bow and arrows—the list went on; I couldn't think about it now. My God, I couldn't even drive, and even if I could, I couldn't communicate. Would I quickly become a bore? None of my patients or staff would understand me when I tried to talk. What would happen to the practice? Would my wife be able to take the changes? Would I lose her too? I began to cry. I don't know how long it had been since I had shed a tear—so stoic in the past—but now the emotions just flooded my being. I don't know how long I cried, but soon a nurse came in and wanted to know if something was wrong. I laughed and shook my head no. What could be wrong?

When one confronts death like this, one instantly becomes humbled by the whole experience of life. That feeling of calm allows one to put the important things of life in order…life, love and family. With that thought it all began to change. I began to put the important things first. My mind or was it God that let me know, regardless, I was going to be all right if I just kept that seed of positive recovery growing.

After all, the tubes were out. I was beginning therapy. The important thing to remember was that the nature or severity of a person's dilemma is not what is important; the person's response to the dilemma is what is important. All the philosophy I had taught over the years was coming back to me now. Could I live my own philosophy?

As I contemplated it all, I was determined I was going to be optimistic, and the result would be positive as well. Sympathy and mercy were a great and compassionate source, but did I need them now? Would just time and the spirit of God get me to the next level? No, I didn't think so. I was going to have to work hard at getting better, just like I've had to work hard at everything all my life.

Take another look at the illustrations I have included to familiarize you with the brain and some of the structures that we are dealing with. The brain, as seen from the side (lateral view) and from above, are the most familiar aspects based on what we have learned from our school textbooks. What I want you to see are the areas of speech, sight and motor ability (movement) and how the left side of the brain controls the right side of the body and vice versa so, the body responds to the opposite side where the brain is injured. My right arm and leg is now paralyzed so the left side of my brain was damaged. See the drawings and illustrations on pages 23, 24 of this book.

Chapter 4

Therapy...Therapy...Therapy!

These are the days of miracles and wonder.
Paul Simon

It was a full day, up before 7:00 A.M., face washed, teeth brushed, dressed, and ready for breakfast. This all began with a nurse dressing me and getting me into the wheelchair. I couldn't even make the wheelchair move correctly, having only one hand to push with. Then I realized I was right-handed before my stroke, and everything had to be done left-handed now.

My teeth were probably as important as anything when it came to personal hygiene. After all, every day of my life I had tried to greet everyone with a smile. My mother had taught me at an early age to take care of my teeth. Before the stroke, I had given little thought to my teeth other than when I was scheduled for a checkup. I brushed them in the morning and after nearly every meal, had them cleaned every three or four months. You might say I took them for granted and did not appreciate my teeth, as I should. Now, sitting in a wheelchair and using the "wrong" hand, just brushing them was an effort. Everyone should try brushing with the opposite hand for a couple of days just to understand a little of what I am about to tell you.

I washed as well as I could; then a nurse came in and asked me if I had go to the toilet before breakfast. This was another embarrassing item I had to deal with, which was actually bigger in my mind than facing the obstacle. One of the most important issues to me and everyone else in my situation was getting on and off the toilet. Of course, I didn't do as I was asked, I did not tell the nurse when I had to use the toilet, as I should have. One day I tried getting up out of bed to go to the toilet. I made it to the door and fell half in and half out of the bathroom door and "could not get up" and had to ring for the nurse. When I tried to tell her what had happened she told me, as my teachers used to tell me in grammar school, that I was lucky I hadn't hurt myself when falling and not to try that again. The nurse said this problem of getting into the bathroom and on and off the toilet was an item the occupational therapist would soon help me with.

Shortly, I was ready. Breakfast was served from 7:30 to 8:30 A.M. This I figured I could handle, even with one hand. After all, there was not much I didn't like to eat. I had a great appetite since childhood and was not very selective about foods as long as they were wholesome. I had eaten about everything in the many foreign countries where I had been lecturing: bugs, worms, whale meat, monkey brains, dog, kangaroo, snake, and even more exotic foods in Africa.

The nurse wheeled me down to the cafeteria. It was full of men and women ranging in ages from about 40 to 90 in wheelchairs, with all types of problems but a great majority were stroke patients, she told me. It was the first time I had seen so many stroke victims together. I later found out that Mercy hospital takes care of rehabilitative-type patients rather than acute patients like most trauma hospitals. Some would get better and be discharged; others would never get any better and would stay in the hospice area of the hospital until their death. Was I in that area? Was I to be one of those statistics?

Right now I was interested in eating. A slot was found for me at the table. The trays were brought to us by some of the nurses and aides. Mine came, and I looked at the little portion, scrambled eggs and bacon with milk to drink. I looked around the room. Some people were eating well and others not so well. Later I found out that their diets and eating habits were monitored like mine. Many had caused their own problems with poor eating habits or had diabetes or heart trouble or were overweight, as I was told by one of the doctors once we became better acquainted.

It was time for my first "meal out" (out of the room) in over two months. I picked up my fork and stared at the small portion that had suddenly gotten larger and larger. I now realized I was no longer the 210 pounds I had been. I was down to 175, the same weight I had been playing eighth grade football. I reached for the milk carton and found I needed both hands to open it, unless I was really good with one hand. I could not talk, so I raised my left hand as if I were in elementary school. Automatically, someone came over to give me some help with the milk carton. Everyone ate. Some talked while others were quiet; they all finished what they could and were wheeled out one by one.

Back in the room, it was time to brush my teeth again and get ready for therapy. It would be my first day at therapy, one of many I would experience. I was taken down to another floor in the wheelchair. When I arrived, I saw that everyone was in a wheelchair. There were nearly 40 people scurrying around; they were in all phases of care, it seemed. The nurse who had brought me down introduced me to the physical therapy staff. Everyone called me Dr. Stump when I was introduced. I guess most knew that I was (or had been) a local doctor and would be familiar with what was happening in the therapy area.

The first person I was introduced to was the department head; she seemed nice and had a big warm smile as she talked. She told me that Kelly would be taking care of me most of the time. The physical therapy area was quite nice—large enough to accommodate nearly fifty patients but still in an intimate setting.

I was soon introduced to Kelly; she was very nice with a kind, warm disposition. Kelly then introduced me to some of the equipment and explained what we were going to try to accomplish each day. She told me I would be coming here for two hours in the morning and two hours in the afternoon.

The first day I was just introduced to the exercise and equipment and spent about five minutes at each station. I was then wheeled over to the next type of therapy, speech therapy. The speech therapy area was smaller but well maintained. Here Kelly introduced me to Nancy, the department head. They spoke privately for a few minutes; then Kelly waved and said she would see me tomorrow. Nancy took me to another room where a man sat at a desk. He was young, about 35, with dark hair and glasses. She introduced him as Mark and then left. I did not get a friendly feeling from him at first, but that may have just been me.

Mark began by explaining what the program was all about and what he would like to see me accomplish. He did not realize that I comprehended only about half of what he said. At one time my mind was like a fine filter with little getting by, and now little would stay. What Mark said was great, hearing all the goals, but meeting them would be something else.

"Speech is commonly affected when the stroke is on the left side of the brain like yours," he said. "I know you're a doctor, but I will explain as much as possible as we go along anyway. There will be times when you understand completely and other times it will seem as though you can't comprehend anything at all. Don't worry just keep trying. Speech disorders do not imply mental incompetence; they indicate that part of your brain cannot function properly." He went on to say there are two basic categories of speech disability: *aphasia* and *dysarthria.*

Aphasia is a disorder of language, both spoken and written, defined in the *Merriam-Webster Dictionary* as: "loss or impairment of the power to use or comprehend words," there are two main types—*expressive* and *receptive*. The expressive type is sometimes called *Broca's aphasia,* and it is the inability to express thoughts verbally. This is the most common form of aphasia. "People with expressive aphasia are not deaf or incompetent," he said, "so I do not have to shout or speak to you as if speaking to a child. This would be both insulting and inappropriate for you. Expressive aphasia is very frustrating for stroke victims and their families. This can often lead to some depression if you let it.

"The other type, receptive aphasia, is also called *Wernicke's aphasia.* It is the inability to understand the spoken or written language. I or anyone else can speak fluently in any language, but the speech does not make sense. This is a much less common disorder and you have the first form," Mark said.

"Now there's one called *dysarthria* and it is a disorder of speech in which the words are slurred and hard to understand. The total voice quality of the individual may be changed, as well as the person's ability to control the volume of his voice. I don't think you have this, but we will know as we go along with our program.

"Speech therapy is usually very effective, especially if you will work at getting improvement as much as possible," he said. He did not know it at this time, but this was one of the effects of this stroke I most wanted to reverse.

I remember that the first exercise that day was to look around the room and identify objects. The first was a clock. I recognized it as something I should know but did not and could not tell him what it was or what time was on its face. I tried to tell what several other items were in the room. I tried and tried but was not capable of doing any better. There was a radio, TV, desk, coat and hat rack, chess game; none of these things could I identify, nor could I utter the simplest words to explain. Mark was happy, as was I, when I managed to say "no," very plainly and we ended our first session.

He then took me to another area on the same floor. According to the sign on the door, it was designated as the OT (occupational therapy) area. I was not as familiar with this as I was with physical therapy. I was introduced to an occupational therapist, Lea. She and Mark spoke privately for a few minutes. Then Mark said goodbye and added we would see a lot of each other over the next few months. We both smiled.

Lea pushed me over to yet another area of the same floor. This area was known as Occupational Therapy (OT) lab, or so it said on the door. There was a brief exchange between Lea and a woman by the name of Susan, who I was soon introduced to and found out later she was the head of the OT department. I was soon introduced to the OT staff—Casey, Michelle, Ed, and Tracy—and was told I would be working with Michelle, a tall South African who really seemed dedicated to doing the OT work she had been trained for while still in South Africa. She was tall for a woman (5′9″ or 5′ 10″) and strong, but not heavy, and very articulate. I liked her instantly. She knew what had to be done and how it was going to be done. "First things first," she would say. "Let's get you over to the area where we practice daily living tasks." Here

Michelle called Ed to come and help. He was big and strong but had a kind and jovial sense of humor. We worked what seemed like an hour on just how to get out of the wheelchair onto another seat, like a toilet!

Over the next few months, Occupational Therapy was more helpful with the practical things I had to learn for daily life. The Physical Therapy (PT) was good for working my muscles because they certainly didn't work on their own anymore. But I was most concerned with speech therapy; this was where we would do the cognitive work. I so desperately wanted to restore my speech. I was humiliated and humbled by the whole stroke incident and the attempt at recovery I was making.

Here I was, a doctor who had been all over the world as a lecturer, spoke Spanish, Japanese, Korean, and some Chinese in conversations, had four doctoral degrees, and was now reduced to being unable to speak any language—not even English. I could not tell time, repeat the alphabet or multiplication tables, or perform any of the basic educational tasks even elementary school children are capable of doing. I was now asked to read nursery school books that I knew I should know and understand...but didn't. Dianne even had cards made up with the ABC's on them for me to study. Was I to start over? Was I to give up? I cried many a night at the hospital when I was alone thinking of my past, present, and future.

What seemed so strange was I could now understand most of what everyone said to me, but I could not articulate a word back to anyone trying to communicate with me. I then determined I was going to give it my all, just as I had done so many times with so many things before. I had to be able to communicate; it was one of my passions. What added even more fuel to the fire was that I could not even write; since the stroke paralysis had affected my right side and I was right handed before. I was starting over there as well!

The frontal lobes are the most highly developed parts of the brain. Human frontal lobes are twice as large as those of other species such as apes. The frontal lobes shape behavior, anticipation, emotion, and—most important—thinking. They are also vital for motor function, planning, and the expression of language. The center for speech expression called *Broca's area* is in the left frontal lobe of right-handers like me.

The frontal lobe also houses the area of the brain where abstract thinking, initiative, and social-inhibitions reside. Stroke survivors who have damage in this area may lose their zest for life. They also become very impulsive in their behavior, unable to tell what is appropriate and what is not. Some stroke survivors swear and say other socially undesirable things. It is not uncommon for stroke survivors who can hardly speak a word to be able to swear a blue streak from frustration even if they didn't swear before. Dianne told me that I had been swearing at the nurses and staff. I was horrified. I was a high school teacher and a former football coach who had never tolerated use of profanity by the staff or players.

If Broca's area is damaged, the person may be unable to speak. As Mark had explained, this is called Broca's expressive aphasia. Most often a person can utter sounds and a few simple words.

For example, my cousin Smitty suffered a stroke after complications from heart surgery several years ago. Smitty and I had been very close since elementary school in Welch, West Virginia. When I went away to the Orient, we lost contact for a few years. When I returned, I learned that Smitty had suffered a stroke and could not walk or talk. I always admired Smitty, for he was another hard-working, talented individual from my family. His wife Carol tells me he is still the same after all the problems from the surgeries and stroke, yet he greets her each morning with a smile. I know that she and my wife could fill volumes concerning the roles and needs of the caretaker, and in a later chapter my wife will put some of those thoughts down for everyone.

Smitty can't speak a word. He can make sounds but I've never heard a word. This was the area of brain damage from his stroke that left him in this condition. He understands the other person and attempts to carry on a conversation. Like the afternoon of my mother's funeral, Smitty and Carol were there. Dianne and I had not seen them for a year and this was a very upsetting time for me. I knew Smitty understood because he had gone through the same thing. Dianne and I asked them if they would have lunch with us. At lunch we carried on a conversation among the four of us but Smitty did not say a single word, just sounds.

Smitty was one of the most determined people I had known. He grew up poor like I did and had to fight and scratch for everything he had. I knew if there was anyway he could have talked he would have been talking.

The staff at Mercy Medical offered me several options of braces and supports. Being in the healing arts I was of the mindset that your body needed to have time to respond to the trauma and to get as strong as possible without the help of braces and supports. Then if it could not, use the supports and braces.

When I was in a wheelchair and without the use of the right arm and leg, it was very difficult to not accept the additional help. My inability to do tasks such as dress myself or even picks up a spoon or uses a knife to spread the butter left me with a depressed feeling of inadequacy. I often wondered if I would regain what the stroke had taken from me.

But, there is hope today for those brain-damaged individuals who are quadriplegics. A study by University of Utah researchers has given hope to those who are wheelchair-bound and have little or no use of their limbs. Published in "brief communications" section of the October 2005 issue of *Nature*, the study reported that paralyzed patients maintained cortical activity in regions that correspond to parts of their bodies that have been paralyzed, contrary to theories and research suggesting cortical reorganization (dysfunction) in these regions. They further believe this finding enables them to continue trying to develop a brain-computer interface that would allow locked-in or high spinal cord-injured patients like the late Christopher Reeves, to operate the wheelchair and other devices by their thought patterns.

I was not wrong in my thinking in this regard. There is new research like the stem cell work being done at Johns Hopkins and other universities. Some countries are actually applying the techniques to the patients with stroke damage who urgently need it and I think this will happen in the United States very soon.

Rehabilitation devices introduced over the past few years are much different than in the past. They now help to restore the function to the weakened area. Devices such as the Saeboflex have helped many patients restore function faster. It is a spring-loaded mechanical brace that enables the patient to pick up objects, dress in the morning and raise an arm above the head, which they normally wouldn't be able to do.

Custom designed for each patient and invented by an occupational therapist, the Saeboflex positions the wrist and finger into extension in preparation for activities such as picking up an object. The extension spring system then assists in reopening the hand to release the object. The device strengthens the muscles of the hand and forearm while being used.

Often stroke patients get discouraged because traditional therapy is a slow process and results do not come quickly or easily for most individuals. Braces, supports, electrical stimulation and devices such as the Saeboflex often do not produce the results as fast as patient's desire. I am fortunate in that regard and understand from being a doctor that recuperating from a neuromuscular condition like a stroke takes much more time than people realize.

Lasers

My friend and professional acquaintance, Margaret Naeser, PhD, associate research professor of neurology at Boston University School of Medicine and licensed acupuncturist in Massachusetts, has conducted research on the use of low-level lasers in the treatment of paralysis and stroke. Subjects showed improvement, and patients with mild to moderate paralysis responded better than those with severe paralysis. The improvements were observed even when the treatments were begun three or four years after the stroke. This research is continuing at several universities. Laser research and laser use in the healing arts is the technological future of medical care. It is now being used in acupuncture, chiropractic and other natural healing arts since the technology has allowed the wattage to be reduced to a therapeutic level.

I received a great deal of benefit from this therapeutic intervention from a personal standpoint. I still use the 500-milliwatt laser each week on my leg and arm that I was loaned by the kind owners and staff of Medical Laser Systems of Connecticut.

Dr. John L. Stump

Neuropathways and Neurofeedback

In the book *Heart Disease, Stroke& High Blood Pressure,* Burton Goldberg and the editors of Alternative Medicine Digest have a section that is very interesting for the stroke patient. In it California therapist Margaret Ayers has been researching brain biofeedback called *Neuropathways EEG Imaging.* This brain research has shown that the imaging may be an effective adjunct in the treatment of serious brain disorders and injury including stroke.

The device used in this technique displays the shape and electrical strength of a patient's brain waves on a computer screen and enables a doctor or therapist to interact with the brain wave pattern.

A study Margaret Ayers conducted in 1987 with 250 individuals with closed head injuries (concussions) showed that long-term brain wave abnormalities resulting from the injury could be improved. The brain constantly emits electrical impulses, registered as waves that indicate the state of health and activity of the brain. In Neuropathway Imaging, gold-plated electrodes are placed on certain areas of the head, corresponding to the brain regions (like Broca's area) where waves need to be corrected or brought into a normal pattern. In effect, the brain is re-trained – this is neuro (brain cells) feedback function – to replace abnormal waves with normal patterns. According to Ayers, once the brain learns the new pattern it becomes permanent. Demonstrated benefits include improvements in short-term memory, concentration, speech, motor skills, energy level, sleep regulation, and emotions.

Let me remind those of you who have had a stroke incident, please don't become discouraged and give up on the therapy, even when the insurance runs out as it did in my case...somehow, continue, continue, continue, because there are those out there who are fighting and willing to help you they just have to know.

DR. JOHN L. STUMP

A STROKE OF MIDNIGHT...

Chapter 5

The Climb Back Up the Hill

Most folks are about as happy as they make up their minds to be.
Abraham Lincoln

After the tours, explanations, and demonstrations of what was to be expected in physical therapy, occupational, and speech therapy at Mercy Medical, it was time to head back to the room. Even though it may not seem like much to some people, it was a big step forward for me. I was getting the chance to attempt the climb back up the hill.

I remembered when we were kids in West Virginia we played a game called King of the Hill. Someone would be designated as king, and then everyone else would have to start at the bottom of the hill and make the steep climb up. Just about the time you were able to get to the top, the king would push you back down. Thirty years I had fought to get to top of the hill of success, and just as I was about to enjoy the fruits of my labor, I was pushed back down by this stroke. I had learned how to win as a child by waiting close to the top and letting the king get into a tussle with someone else, then slip to the top and push them both off. Now I had to make that slow climb back to the top of this hill of health and wait for the opportunity to succeed again.

Back in my room, I was alone and wondering what was going to happen. Here I was, only able to sit in a wheelchair. Dianne was left to take care of everything: my patients, our office, the employees, the Alabama Oriental Studies Institute, our students, my lecture schedule, and our home on the bay. Could she manage all of that? I knew we had some good employees, but was this asking too much? There was nothing I could do but try to let her know I would do the best I could to get back to helping her with upkeep of everything.

That night Dianne came up to the hospital in Daphne. God was I glad to see her! I tried to tell her about the different therapies and what they had explained to me. Of course, I could not communicate with speech at the time, but I was still able to be emphatic. I tried to "grunt" and point with as much feeling as possible. I know it was difficult for her, but she was very patient and kind in the practically one-sided conversation.

For the next few weeks, most of the day was filled with therapy—three sessions in the morning and three in the afternoon instead of the normal two they first had scheduled. I did not know that the sessions were shorter at first then gradually got longer as my stamina improved. Usually I would get back to my room about 3:30 P.M. and rest until 4:30, then get ready for dinner. After dinner it was free visiting time until bedtime, about 8–9 P.M.

I did not know that Dianne and Randa, my private secretary at the office, had made a visiting schedule. I had many people wanting to visit, Dianne said, but I could not talk and was very emotional when I tried. She and Randa felt it would be best if only a few came up at one time.

They made the schedule to accommodate the need. I would have a few visitors each evening. I'm not sure they realized I didn't know any of them at that time, but I really appreciated their coming to see me, and I could tell from the inflection of their voices they were sincere in their feelings of wanting me to get better. But I really didn't understand what they were talking about.

Bill Scott, a former nuclear submarine sailor who had been a patient, became Dianne's helper. He is a big strapping lad who had the same role taking care of his wife, who was wheelchair-bound, and knew of the many items I would require. He and Mike, our neighbor, whom Dianne had called the night of the stroke really were a great help to Dianne and me throughout my entire hospital stay, even though I was unaware of most of what they were doing until later.

I did not realize I had lost more than thirty pounds since being hospitalized and weighed about 175 pounds now. It is not, however, a diet I would recommend; the Atkins Diet or "The Zone" would be much easier! I was not even concerned about weight or food at this time. Actually, food was never a high priority for me. I remember when I was in China and India going for days without much more than a few grains of rice or a few berries or a root to chew. This was a part of the Buddhist training at the time, but I cared more about the physical and philosophical training than eating. I could eat whatever or whenever I was told even if there were days between meals—and there were sometimes several days.

Actually, I was more concerned about what I was going to do about my situation, realizing my life, as I had known it had now ended and I was beginning a new phase. I was no longer the world-traveling lecturer, "Professor Go" as I was called in Orient for all of the "globetrotting" I did. The stroke had come five days before Dianne and I were to leave for New Zealand, where I was to do a presentation on sports chiropractic at an international sports medicine conference. This was pretty well the end of the lectures and presenting research at world conferences, I thought. If I went anywhere now it would be in a wheelchair.

After another week, Dianne came in one night and said, "Mike and Bill have volunteered to come up and take care of you while I go to Chad's wedding." Well, I had forgotten this important event in the months after the stroke. Chad, our older son, was getting married. God, I wanted to go. I choked back the tears as she told me the plans that evening. Randa was going with her, she said.

Randa was a trooper; she could do anything and go anywhere. Her husband Ed was the same. They never blinked an eye, I'm sure, when Dianne asked Randa to go to Delaware with her to Chad's wedding. Dianne, Randa, and Sue (Mike's wife) all worked together in the office and were very good friends. They went everywhere together: shopping, house tours, art shows, everything. So it didn't surprise me that she would call on Randa to help her out. Sue was our office manager and would take care of things on the business front.

The fear of Dianne leaving was just about overwhelming for me. I could not imagine a week without Dianne. She took care of everything. I didn't even know the medication I was taking. She came to the hospital every day with a smile and looking so beautiful. This was going to max me out, I was sure, but I didn't say anything…I couldn't!

I should have known better, but I guess in this condition I was not thinking very clearly to have thought Dianne would have left me uncared for. Instead, she left me in the hands of two very capable men, Mike, a "McGuyver" who could fix anything and Bill, the big, old ex-submariner. He and Mike were both patients with occasional back problems. Little did I know, but Dianne had made a time schedule for Bill and Mike to come to the hospital and stay during visiting hours until her return the following week.

They were both good company. They helped me in and out of the bathroom and even helped me some with the homework the speech therapist had given me. The only thing they could not help me with was the abandoned and forsaken feeling I would get. This feeling had to be left behind; I could not keep this emotion. Was this going to be a regular thing now, for me to feel left behind and left out?

Because I was unable to make the trip, on doctor's orders, I would miss a very important event in the life of one of our children. There were a lot of emotions tied to this separation and trip to the Eastern Shore of Maryland and Delaware for Dianne. All kinds of things would go through my mind at night. Would Dianne return and want a divorce because she saw I was a handicap to her for the rest of our marriage? How could I now provide for her in the manner that she deserved? I was now only half a man; what could I do for her intimately? Would I be able to perform sexually now? This was a question I would later discuss at length with the doctor. These and many similar thoughts would race through my mind at night, and I would cry myself to sleep.

The week was a long one for Bill and Mike, having to take turns sitting with me. There would be hours when I would just sit and stare into emptiness. Bill once said, "What are you sitting there thinking about?" I could not answer him; I really wasn't thinking of anything: it was like my mind was in a holding pattern trying to buy time to put my thoughts or something together. Later he said I would just sit and look off into the distance somewhere, like I was a thousand miles away. I still don't know whether I was thinking of anything or not, but I guess my brain needed time to repair the damage that had been done by the stroke.

Dianne and Randa came back a week later telling horror stories about driving around the Baltimore-Washington

Beltway and through the cities of Baltimore and Washington D.C. They told about how gorgeous the gowns were and what a great wedding it had been. All told, they said they had a wonderful time, which I wished I had not missed.

Was I going to tell Dianne how much I had missed her and how frightening it had been the first three or four days without her? The days were not so bad because I had the therapy sessions and the other patients to be with. Then Mike or Bill would come up, but after they left the nights were 48 hours long, it seemed! I think she could tell right away because when we were alone and I tried to say something to her about her being gone and the trip, I would just break down. I don't know why; I just would. It seemed like the emotion of just having her back beside me was overwhelming. I could not imagine not having her with me now; what would I do? Was she going to tell me that she had decided separation and divorce was better at this point?

After a few days I got over that emotional hurdle. Now I had to find out how much longer the doctors were going to keep me in the hospital and what I had to accomplish to get them to allow me to go home. I worked very hard at therapy each day. The physical therapy was easier for me than the speech therapy, but little by little, day-by-day, a few words began to come out of my mouth the correct way. I could also walk down the hall with the help of the therapist, and then one day I could take a few steps without the therapist. I was actually standing and walking a few steps on my own. This progress continued for the next few weeks.

Dianne and I had also decided to ask the doctor if I could begin acupuncture treatment. The doctor was coming to the clinic each Monday, Wednesday, and Friday to see patients for me; he could stop at the hospital on his way back to Pensacola and treat me. Dianne agreed to ask Dr. Alfred

Chance, the hospital director, if the acupuncture treatment would be permitted. The next day when she came in, she said it was all arranged and we would begin soon. Dr. Chance even said he would like to observe the treatment. I suppose Dr. Chance thought I needed all the help I could get. Later in the *Integrative Medicine Section* I will give part of the formula and why acupuncture, chiropractic and proper nutrition was so successful in getting me up and around so quickly.

Other Plights...

Rather than give a detailed recitation of my daily progress, I will give you some of the highlights and low points of the climb back onto the horse that threw me. I will take you through an account of some of the progress I could see happening and some things not so promising.

For instance, I didn't know until I was later told, my bed had to be equipped with a special buzzer that notified the front desk when I tried to get up at night when no one was around and go to the toilet. I could not walk, so I would end up falling and knocking things down. I was like a bull in a china shop the nurses said. I had no balance, no coordination.

One time I remember falling so hard it scared the patients in the room next door. I guess I didn't yet realize I couldn't walk. My entire right side felt extremely heavy, as if I were carrying a concrete arm and leg. I just couldn't seem to understand the stroke had left me a paraplegic: only half of me functioned. This made it very difficult to stand or to get around, especially in confined areas, because my leg would swing out beyond a normal swing pattern, and my foot would catch or hit something. It took many months of physical therapy to retrain that muscle pattern. Even to this day my leg will revert to that pattern if I get tired or try to hurry.

This is still the case five years later; my right side still feels very heavy. I can move better and have found ways to compensate for the nonfunctioning muscles of my right arm and right leg. At some point after the installation of the buzzer on my hospital bed, I finally accepted the fact I was incapacitated and stopped trying to get out of it without help.

Dianne came each day and wheeled me to dinner and up and down the halls where we would try to converse. Later she told me that outside of the shock I provided the staff from time to time with the profanity that came pouring out of my mouth during some visits, I had been a model patient. Of course, this I couldn't help and was not even aware of for months. This concerned me very much, but the doctor had told Dianne it is sometimes normal to regress back in language development and she should not be concerned at this point. Anything that comes out of my mouth was progress, he said!

After a little more than a month in therapy, I first noticed my vision began to clear, and I began to regain feeling in the right side of my face. I didn't slobber and bite my lip nearly as much as I had in the first few months. Even now, five years later, I still occasionally bite my lip when I try to talk or chew too fast.

In January, I was able to extend my right shoulder, where there had been no movement since the stroke. By February, there was some movement and feeling beginning in my right leg. In March, I could lift my right upper arm; the deltoid muscle was beginning to respond. In April, feeling began to return to my right elbow. In May, I noticed some feeling and movement in my right hand; there was some independent movement of each finger, but not much. So now I could see some progress occurring each week and each month but when could I go home?

I was making progress in all of my therapy. I was most pleased with my speech therapy because I had resigned myself to the fact that I could live with whatever physical difficulties I had suffered, but I could not think of not being able to communicate with those around me. After all, I had spent the last 25 years becoming a prominent speaker on the sports medicine, acupuncture and chiropractic circuit. Now I was not able to speak an intelligible word.

In May, however, we experienced a setback. Blue Cross dropped my coverage for the physical therapy and occupational therapy. Dianne was told that if I was to continue treatment, the only solution was to seek help from Vocational Rehabilitation Services of Alabama. That was a big blow to the effort. I had not realized that every day was a concern for their dollar and not my progress. I had always been a very hard worker in any effort I attempted, and it was the same now. I was making good progress, but that didn't matter to the insurance company. It was like the ride on the little bucking horse when I was a child: I didn't understand the correlation between inserting a coin and the length of the ride. Just about the time I was getting the hang of riding it, it was over. It was that way with my therapy: now that I was beginning to make progress, I was being cut off.

Dianne was wonderful. She intervened and arranged for another managed-care insurance to take over at that point. My therapy continued for the next several months. Everyone could see and would tell me how well I was doing. However, the progress did not seem as good to me. I could still walk just a few steps, utter only a few words and identify a few more simple items. I could understand what was said to me and felt I understood more clearly what my cognitive requests were from the therapist, but I just could not make my body respond.

I had heard for years about mind over matter, and at one time my mind had been as strong as my body. But neither mind nor matter was responding any faster than nature would let it at that time. If the concept that mind over matter worked, it must have had a flaw now because my mind seemed like a piece of Swiss cheese. I knew many mental centering techniques that I had learned at Zen temples in Japan and China but nothing seemed to help. At least there didn't seem to be any miracles occurring then for me. Later a physician on duty in the Emergency Room the night they brought me in told me neither he nor the other doctor thought I would make it through the night. So, maybe there was a miracle that I just wasn't aware of happening. God had not finished with me yet!

This was going to be an incredibly long and difficult journey. I had been used to being an athlete, being able to master something after being shown once or twice. I remembered going with a group of friends to Vail, Colorado to ski. I had never been skiing in the real powder of the West before, always on the icy slopes of the East. They told me to stay on the beginners' slope the first morning until I got used to the skis, snow, and slopes. I stayed there for one run then went to the top of the mountain, to the black-diamond slopes that were more of a challenge. It was the same with just about anything I attempted. But I could see this was going to be different. Those other things were just a warm-up; this stroke rehabilitation was going to be a real-life challenge.

The worst physical problem that could not be overcome was the constant *spasticity* in my right arm and my right leg. This condition, I was told, was uncontrollable muscle tightness in the affected area—in my case the right arm and leg. It is supposedly a common physical response to an injury to the brain. The brain loses control over the contraction of the muscle, leaving the muscle to contract independently and involuntarily. The muscle does not and cannot obey the nervous system's signals to relax, and remains in a stiff, taut, knotted state. In stroke patients, spasticity can be both harmful and helpful, somewhat like a yin and yang state. It can remain in painful tightness of joints, particularly the shoulder, like mine, and the hip. In my hip and knee the spasticity caused more extension, making it harder to bend the hip and knee. I walked slowly and very awkwardly at first.

The spasticity has now subsided slightly, but it took the best part of three years to walk with only a slight limp. The spasticity continues to be my number-one worst stroke result. I have overcome the weakness of the muscles by going to the Homestead Wellness Center in Fairhope and working out every other day. The muscles involved have gotten stronger and the surrounding *synergistic* muscles, (muscles that help the primary muscles, affected by the stroke) have gotten stronger as well.

In June of the following year, I was surprised when Dianne told me our business had won one of the Eastern Shore Chamber of Commerce awards for that year. There was to be a big awards ceremony for the town businesses in several categories. We had worked very hard for the past ten years at remodeling the building, and the property had been spruced up with a new paint job and awnings, a new parking area, new shrubs, and a new sign. Thus, I suppose everyone could see the improvements of the office at 401 North Section Street in Fairhope.

Dianne told me I would need to get into a suit if I was going to be dressed properly for the awards ceremony. She had arranged for me to be checked out of Mercy Medical Hospital for four hours. Little did I know, but the doctors were using this as a way to help them assess my progress up to this stage in treatment. Dianne came to the hospital that evening with all my duds: shoes, white shirt, suit and even cufflinks. I felt odd trying to get ready. I could not tie my tie, couldn't tie my shoes—would I have to have Dianne or someone else dress me for the rest of my life? I began to weep. I did not know why; it just happened.

She wheeled me out of the hospital and got me into the car and off we went. It felt really good being out of the hospital for the first time in over four months. Riding in the car felt strange, much like being on my boat, but I didn't tell Dianne for fear she would take me back to the hospital. We arrived at the Fairhope Civic Center, where the ceremony was to be held. She got the wheelchair from the trunk of the car and finally got me into the building. I was greeted by a lot of my old friends—at least I assumed they were old friends. I knew that I knew them, but for the life of me I could not remember their names. It was strange. I knew I was there, but it was like I was still in a time warp, with the people and the things happening all around me, yet I was not really a part of it.

The ceremony began and there was a lot happening I could not keep up with. After what I guess was a short time, Dianne said that was our cue to go to the podium for the presentation. She wheeled me up to the front. I asked her to lock the chair so it wouldn't roll. I wanted to stand and say how much we appreciated the award. I had not walked since the stroke except a few steps in therapy. I stood and slowly took the three steps that were necessary. Then I tried to say what I felt. Now I was not sure I could utter a simple thank you. I opened my mouth and started just as I had done on so many occasions before and much to my surprise the proper words started to come, slowly but surely I muttered a sentence or two.

The people seemed to be on the edge of their chairs, but I'm sure it wasn't for the same reasons I had always looked for in the past at my lectures. They had all heard I wasn't supposed to be able to walk or talk, or even to be alive, yet here I was standing in front of them getting ready for who knows what. To that point I had not been able to articulate more than three or four intelligible words.

Dianne later told me I did manage a few short sentences along with a clear "thank you" that I was trying so desperately to get out. We took the long way back to the hospital at my request, but we arrived way too early in my estimation.

Dianne came in later that week and told me that the doctors had agreed I would be able to go home soon. Damn, did that make me happy! Not that they didn't take good care of me and try their best, but I missed being home, seeing Dianne in the kitchen, our kids, their messy rooms, and the views of Mobile Bay at sunset. I promised I would do whatever they asked—just let me go home! I knew at that time I wouldn't have been a good prisoner.

It was all the steps we had at home the doctors and therapists were concerned about. We lived on the bay, and the flood control law stated our house had to be at least 13 feet above a certain level. But how would I manage 15 steps every time I had to go in and out of the house? I could hardly climb five at the therapy center. What if there was a fire; how would Dianne get me down?

I persuaded the doctors to let me try getting up and down the steps. I had been doing real well in PT, and I had walked a few steps at the awards ceremony. We had a nice stairway with good handrails, so I was pretty sure I could do it if I had too. The next day they let me out of the hospital to go home with Dianne to see if I could climb the stairs. This was a sure test for me. I had climbed four or five steps at the hospital as part of my PT rehab but never 15.

We got to the house and it had never looked so good. It was a beautiful day on the bay; we could see for miles from our entrance. I got out of the car and Dianne helped me to the handrail at the steps. I was still not able to use my right side much at that point. I looked up the steps; they had never looked so high and steep. The staircase reminded me of the first level of Ayers Rock in Australia, sheer rock straight up. I had made Dianne climb with me when we were there a few years back. Now the tables were turned; I was the one having to be pushed to do the climbing.

I took hold of the rail and started my ascent. The first few steps were fine but after that each step became harder. After ten I was beginning to wonder if I could stand, let alone climb. Dianne saw the look on my face and asked if I would like to sit. I didn't want to give up, but I was afraid that if I didn't, I would fall and make matters worse. I sat down on the step and began tearing up, another response I couldn't prevent. But I was afraid if I couldn't make it they would make me stay at the hospital. This crying came on very easily and without warning; I had never been emotional before, but I sure was now.

After a few minutes I stood and said, "Let's give it another go." That time I climbed the next five steps without difficulty. We entered the front door, and when I crossed the threshold I thought about just staying there and refusing to return to the hospital. We spent a few minutes just slowly moving from one room to the next, to see if there were areas to support myself and to see what had to be done to make the house accommodating to my stroke requirements.

I knew the bathroom would have to be made ready first. I could hardly go an hour without having to urinate; the frequency alone was exhausting. This was one of the reasons I had tried to get up on my own at the hospital at first. This too has gradually improved over the years.

There were a few difficult spots that I knew would have to be changed, but I didn't say a word. Several had passed since we entered the door; now I was ready to try the descent. I got to the top and looked down the steps. Was I going to be able to do it? Actually going down the steps was more difficult than going up. I had no control of my right hand and leg. I almost fell several times, but finally I was at the landing and had only three more steps to go. I continued, and then I was on the ground. I had made it! I noticed that just coming down the steps I was in almost as much of a sweat as I had been after running the Marine Corps Marathon in Washington, D.C., some years back. I guess it was the tense emotion rather than just the muscular effort that had really brought the sweat out.

For the next several hours I kept practicing until I could go up and down without stopping. I won't say how many attempts that was, but Dianne said she got tired just watching. When we returned to the hospital, I felt more confident knowing I could get in and out of the house in an emergency.

That weekend I was released from Mercy Medical Hospital and told to return Mondays, Wednesdays, and Fridays for my outpatient therapy. This was the best news I had heard in the past four or five months.

It was the summer solstice, and I had noticed I was able to isolate the intrinsic muscles of the right hand—a little progress in this area and this made me happy. With the extension of my thumb still not cooperating, I seemed to have a ways to go. There was still no grip in the right hand. On the first of July of that first year, I went with Dianne to the grocery store. As I was pushing the cart, which helped me with support, I could all of a sudden keep a grip on the handle of the cart…victory, another little sign of progress. So I want to emphasize that while to me the progress was slow, everyone else seemed to think I was making good improvement both physically and emotionally.

Just don't give up, I told myself; *continue the journey as long as it may take.* An old Chinese saying comes to mind here: *"The journey of a thousand miles begins with the first step."* This was certainly a journey of a thousand miles and slow steps and one at a time, were about all that could be taken. I knew this was a long, slow journey, but what was the alternative—to sit in a wheelchair and feel sorry for myself? Not me! I wanted to at least be able to say that I had given it my best effort.

Here again I was faced with the problem of depression. *Depression* was a word that had never been in my active vocabulary. Some of my patients talked about how they had been in a state of depression for months, but this was something I had never experienced myself. Now I could understand what might drive them to such a state of mind. But I was convinced I could overcome the affects of this stroke, and I was not going to let it drive me into depression at this point in the rehabilitation.

Depression can be so bad for some people that they are practically *catatonic* (the ultimate withdrawal seen in forms of major depression), a state that many people either enter or approach after a stroke. They get so bad they are often chaotic and totally unable to participate in therapy. In these cases, there are often inadequate skills at the bedside by the nurses and aids that are unprepared for such crisis management of these patients. In most cases they over medicate them and hope they get better with time. However, usually these people are soon seen by the psychiatrist but, nowadays a patient may see a "therapist specializing in psychology or social problems" and, when needed, the psychiatrist just for the medication.

It is no wonder that these patients suffered depression and uncontrollable swings in emotion from tears to laughter. I myself suffered several of these mood swings but thankfully mine stayed on the light side compared to many.

This is where prayer comes into play in sickness and recovery. Even though many of the scientific studies do not support the benefit of prayer and healing, throughout history people have shown their support of each other through this means. The very thought that others are praying and have prayed for your recovery motivates you even more to fight for survival. This again is where body, mind and spirit cannot be separated. I think this aspect of science is still ill equipped to measure the benefits of prayer and praying for the person.

I want to thank all those that shared their prayers, reflections and thoughts for recovery of me during those days when even I was not aware of my future.

Integrative Medicine and Stroke Care

For the past 25 years I've had to straddle the fence between two worlds, Western medicine and Eastern medicine. Since returning from the Orient (Japan, China, and Korea), where I studied acupuncture, I have tried to blend the practice of the two. In my personal practice there was no problem. I followed the same basic procedure used in the Orient for most patients. But could that be done for me now at this hospital in conservative Alabama?

It is not clear when the development and use of acupuncture really began. Legend has it that it was first discovered more than 5,000 years ago in China. Some authorities refute this and say they can prove it is more like 10,000 years old. Regardless of the exact date, it is steeped in antiquity. At a time, when wars were fought with knives, spears, bows and arrows, a strange phenomenon occurred: The monks who cared for injured soldiers recorded where the soldiers and warriors were injured. Later it was observed that wounds in certain places allowed aches and pains in other places to disappear.

Over hundreds of years, this information was recorded, categorized, and systematized into what is now known as *Traditional Oriental Medicine.* This led the Chinese somewhere along this timeline to discover a human energy system that communicates energetic information throughout the total body. This energy system became known as *qi,* and is also known as life force, *ki, prana,* or life energy, as well as several other terms in different countries.

From a scientific viewpoint, one problem with energy medicine is the challenge of creating the concrete proof that it exists; many scientists agree that it does and yet just as many scientists disagree that enough proof is in to prove human energy exists. But I am a believer!

The discovery of the human energy system and Traditional Oriental Medicine eventually led to the development of acupuncture as we know it today, a procedure by which the body's energy is altered by stimulating—with needles, electricity, ultrasound, laser, etc.—specific points along twelve major pathways that are known as *meridians.* Each of these meridians passes through a specific organ of the body, such as the lungs, large intestine, heart, liver, stomach, etc. The entire system is interconnected so the *qi,* or life energy, travels from one meridian to the next, circulating throughout the body (much like the blood). These meridians interact with a number of more concentrated energy fields called *chakras* to help maintain our body's homeostasis, the tendency of the body to try to maintain normal internal stability.

In acupuncture treatment, tiny specialized needles are inserted into the body at specific sites (*acupuncture points*) to increase energy (*tonification*) or to decrease energy (*sedation*). Over the many hundreds of years that acupuncture has been practiced, points have become known that will eliminate pain, cause anesthesia of a body part, help cure illness, help eliminate addictions, and increase energy. In general, acupuncture has been used for most general problems for thousands of years with good success.

Increasingly, more people in the United States are using acupuncture as a viable means of treatment without using drugs or surgery. In the Far East, however, I saw the perfect use of integrative medicine. Western-trained doctors and surgeons would work side by side with acupuncturists and *tuina* (manipulation) specialists, like chiropractors, in the hospitals for the benefit of the patient. The World Health Organization has to date cited more than 104 conditions that can be treated using acupuncture procedures.

From Oriental medicine, I've learned humans are a part of the natural world and illness can be seen as a disruption of the environment in which we reside. Through the eyes of my grandmother and Dr. Fukinbara, my *sensei,* and the many other master healers I have studied under through the years, I've been able to understand my patients better. All patients come in with a story of who they are and why they are in the office for that particular problem at that particular time in their life.

I have spent the last 30 years not just discovering and mastering acupuncture but learning to integrate these eastern methods into my western chiropractic practice. In some ways, my journey to establish integrative medicine has mirrored the growth of acupuncture itself in America. I was one of a handful of Americans who knew how to use acupuncture in

1972. I was now to see the reward as I neared the end of the century. I was now about to receive acupuncture in a very conservative area of the country where I had brought acupuncture over twenty years earlier. I had taught over 50 physicians acupuncture in Alabama and now I needed it myself. To treat stroke patients is not new in the practice of acupuncture. On the following pages I have included some information regarding its use.

The *Great Compendium of Acupuncture and Moxibustion* from 1601 is a treasure trove of medical ditties. In it was the following example for "difficult" illnesses. This particular stanza prescribes acupuncture points for what western medicine would call a stroke.

> ***Four limbs flaccid,***
> ***Attacked by evil wind,***
> ***Eyes rough, difficult to open,***
> ***attacked by diseases,***
> ***Spirit confused, tired, not speaking,***
> ***Fengchi and Hegu are needled.***

Before we continue my story, here's an excerpt from a recent medical review on stroke written by Francine Rainone, PhD, MD, Director of Community Palliative Care, Department of Family Medicine, Montefiore Medical Center, Bronx, New York.

"*My intention here is to utilize most of the available literature to review the topic of acupuncture for stroke. The purpose of the review is not to access the evidence for efficiency so much as to think through the issue as an acupuncturist and a researcher.*

In the People's Republic of China, acupuncture is widely used as an adjunct in the treatment for stroke. In the

United States it is almost never used. In general, therapies are investigated in this country because they elicit physiological mechanisms that suggest potential efficiency and/or because there is compelling clinical evidence of their effectiveness. Numerous studies demonstrate that acupuncture induces physiological changes that promote healing after ischemic and hemorrhagic brain injury, but the clinical evidence is mixed. A recent review concluded that there is no additional benefit to administering acupuncture as a part of a comprehensive rehabilitation program following stroke. This conclusion is premature and needs further investigation."

I recently wrote a chapter in an acupuncture textbook on the use and effectiveness of acupuncture in stroke that some of you might wish to read (see ***Electroacupuncture - by David Mayor, 2007)***. In this text I outline in detail what the acupuncturist must know and understand about the treatment of the stroke victim. As we go along I will give you some of the highlights of my acupuncture treatment process that I underwent for the effects of stroke.

Chiao Shun-fa, at a North China County hospital in the Peoples Republic of China, first introduced the Acupuncture Scalp points in 1971, just before I went to China to study acupuncture. I met Chiao Shun-fa in 1982. His investigation of 1,046 cases handled by the Chishan County People's Hospital in Shansi province showed that needling certain points on the scalp was very useful in treating paralysis caused by pathological changes in the brain by stroke. The effectiveness of this therapy also relates to the location where the brain injury occurred and how much time has elapsed before acupuncture treatment begins; the shorter the time the better the result. The right side of my body was the side with the paralysis so the left side of the scalp was the area of concentration of the acupuncture.

My scalp needling continued for the first two weeks every other day in the motor/sensory and the language areas, the upper point of the motor and sensory areas seemed to be especially helpful. After the two-week period, full body acupuncture was incorporated into the treatment plan. This is a long process, not something that you can do in 3 or 4 treatments. It took me about 12-15 treatments before I could tell some progress was being made.

Acupuncture, Chiropractic, Applied Nutrition and a great deal of sports injury treatment was my practice before the stroke and this seemed to be the way I was going to get my rehabilitation to where I could help myself more every week.

I had been told I had a very big practice, one of the largest in the state of Alabama and in the United States. I saw numerous patients each day and averaged about 500+ patients each week. The clinic needed someone who understood how to care for that many people at that rate. It was non-stop treatment from 7 in the morning until 7 at night 5 days a week.

I remember doing an internship rotation with Dr. Bill Bahan and his brothers at their clinic in Derry, New Hampshire. They saw nearly a thousand patients each week but there were 4 or 5 doctors plus all the dozens of staff. I did another rotation with Drs. Pierce and Stillwagon of Monongahela, Pennsylvania. They had a large practice with several interns and a very specialized technique that I had studied and used at the Palmer College of Chiropractic Clinic. I met Dr. Vernon Pierce and asked if I could become an intern under his and Dr. Stillwagon's direction. Working in a fantastic healing atmosphere like these clinics was great experience. I also interned at the Spears Hospital in Denver, Colorado. At the time, it was the only chiropractic hospital in the United States. I had the opportunity to see many cases few chiropractors get a chance to see in their private practice while working there at Spears Hospital.

I was beginning to cut back some when I moved to Alabama in 1987; this way I would have more time to teach. I learned I could affect more people by teaching more doctors than treating one patient at a time. I had started seeing patients only half a day on Fridays, because that way I could leave a little earlier when I lectured somewhere like in New York City, New Haven, Chicago, or San Francisco. I had always had a large and busy practice; at one time I had nine or ten assistants and four associate doctors working with me. When I practiced on the Eastern Shore of Maryland, my wife and I had three offices and started at 6:30 A.M. seeing the farmers and the early patients that had to go to work. I would work until about eight every evening. Some nights my staff didn't get out of the office until 9 P.M. Now, I know that it was too much for everyone but I was doing what I wanted; I loved taking care of the patients.

Dianne had put the practice at 401 Professional Centre in Fairhope, Alabama up for sale in the year 2000 after the stroke. She had several doctors that came in to try to take the practice, to keep things going until she found a buyer but it seemed impossible to find a doctor that could take on such a task. The doctors and therapists at Mercy Medical Hospital told her I would never be able to walk or talk, let alone see patients again. More than likely, I would be confined to a wheelchair and would have very poor speech, if any. In the beginning they really didn't give her much hope for my survival at all. Dianne said very little about all the problems this was causing with the business. She tried to keep all the negative effects away from me while I was in the hospital and during my first days at home.

Monday, Wednesday, and Friday without fail, after my chiropractic and acupuncture treatments, I could see more progress, especially with my energy. I felt more vibrant and ready to take on more each day. The physical response was still slow, but I was more concerned with the cognitive functions of my body. Dianne talked with Dr. Alfred Chance, the director of Mercy Medical and asked if the hospital would make sure I was getting the needed vitamin and mineral supplements that should be prescribed. Supplements I had not taken for months, since having the stroke. I had always followed a good diet and taken dietary whole food supplements due to depletion of good soil to grow nutritious foods in this country (a belief that I still have today).

As a matter of fact, I had never missed a day of work due to illness or sickness in 25 years—a couple of days due to injuries and broken bones but never sickness. I wanted to be sure that my body was getting what it needed for repair. I had not received any nutritional supplements at all in the time I was in either hospital in the last several months. Was this because of the medications or because doctors didn't believe a stroke patient needed the additional nutritional support? I still am not sure what their reasoning was but I know that the Southern diet has been implicated in several studies of stroke.

A 2005 AARP Bulletin published the HEALTH ALERT... 'Is the Stroke Belt Moving'? People who live in Georgia, North Carolina, South Carolina and Alabama are twice as likely to die from a stroke as the average American is to die from a stroke. In 1968, the high-risk area was centered near Atlanta, according to George Howard of the University of Alabama, a leading stroke expert and researcher. Another high-risk area has now developed toward Arkansas...former President Clinton's (another Cardiovascular Disease victim) home.

A recent study published in 2004 by the *Journal of Nutrition* showed that individuals taking a daily multivitamin supplement experienced fewer heart attacks than those who did not. It just made logical sense to me that if you got good results with a general multivitamin you would get better results with more specific supplementation.

The recommendations for me included several specific vitamins, minerals and herbs that I was on four months, and then changed according to my progress. The progress was monitored by my blood analysis and a trace mineral analysis every four months for the first year.

All these vitamins, minerals, herbs and enzymes and were 100% organic whole food supplements from Standard Process Company in Palmyra, Wisconsin. Dr. Royal Lee, a dentist and researcher, founded this company nearly 100 years ago. He had investigated the diets of thousands of people all over the world to try to determine why some cultures had good teeth and few cavities and other cultures had bad teeth and a lot of cavities. Note that this research was done in the early 1900s. Since that time the Standard Process Company has been dedicated to the 100% whole food philosophy and people's health. I had used their products in my practice since first beginning nutritional work with my patients in 1976; now here I was in need of the same supplement schedule as many of the patients to help repair my body.

When I returned from the Orient in 1981 I wanted to have an apothecary and health food store were I could recommend the type and kind of food and nutrition the patients needed. At the time there was no source for this on the Eastern Shore of Maryland or Delaware. That is the reason we started the Zen Den & Natural Foods Loft in Delmar, Delaware. In doing the research to try to find organic foods and natural supplements I came across the Standard Process Company and found it had a sterling reputation. I have been with them ever since.

My recovery process was going to be a long one, but I felt I basically had two choices. One was to not do anything and let nature take its course. The other was to do all I could to see if I could help effect a change on the improvement of the stroke symptoms that had occurred. I chose the second way, to give my body all it needed: exercise, vitamins, minerals, enzymes and the prescribed meditation, in order to assist what could be helped and speeded up. All these factors together are some of the reasons why I believe I have been so successful in a relatively speedy recovery; of course no recovery is ever speedy enough for the person suffering the aftermath of a stroke.

Let me say I wouldn't be here today if it weren't for the great medical efforts provided by the hospital and the doctors on staff at Thomas Hospital in Fairhope. In no way am I saying that medication is not necessary in the care of a stroke victim. Because I did have such good medical care at Thomas Hospital and at Mercy Medical Hospital I was able to begin the preventative plan to help reduce the need for additional medication and extensive medical support.

I had learned while working in Chinese hospitals that many natural treatments are used instead of medications to try to enhance the natural response and decrease the cost of patient care. The Chinese are very frugal and use herbs, vitamins and minerals initially. Only when it's necessary are medications and surgery brought into the picture, as opposed to the western way of using medication superfluously in many cases.

Dianne and I agreed that we would work tirelessly to see that all was done naturally and without drugs as much as possible and that exercise, diet, supplements and a great spiritual direction would guide my recovery.

It seems like the Chinese are light years ahead of Americans when it comes to preventive Medicine. It's time to change the way doctors predict heart and stroke problems. Doctors now estimate a person's risk of heart attack or stroke by looking at a combination of risk factors, like high blood pressure, high cholesterol, smoking, age, diabetes, and family history.

But, that's old practice; the Koreans, Japanese and Chinese that I worked with in the Olympics were very concerned about heart and circulatory problems. If you wanted to identify athletes who have heart disease and circulatory problems, don't look at risk factors; look at where the plaque is or may be…in the arteries.

It would be best if we would start routinely doing a CT scan on each person over the age of 45 to directly measure the artery-clogging plaque, or ultrasounds that will measure directly the narrowing of the arteries. Prevention needs to become the top priority.

Chapter 6

Another Mountain

I've learned that everyone wants to live on the mountaintop, but all the happiness and growth seems to occur while climbing up.
Author unknown

I was released from rehab and told I would continue my therapy on an outpatient basis for another few months. I was glad to be back home; four months in the hospital was more than enough. However, I found my share of obstacles and challenges at home as well. The first thing I noticed was the last thing that I had remembered when being carried down from the house to the ambulance, the steps. Fifteen from bottom to top was a real struggle to get up but even more coming down. From the trip out here earlier, I knew I could do it, but what a struggle! I conquered it by making it a part of my therapy each day to have to climb the stairs four times up and down, morning and afternoon. It's like learning to run a marathon: you master three miles at a time then put them all together.

I had to try to get around as well as possible. Learning the layout of the house again from a different perspective was another obstacle. I had to learn how to negotiate my house in the wheelchair as well as a walker. Learning to use the toilet and shower took as long as anything. We had to get a new adapted toilet seat with handles on the sides. One thing I never learned well enough at occupational therapy was how to take a shower alone. Dianne always had to get in and help me—there had to be a golden lining somewhere in this stroke story!

Also, railings had to be mounted on our back stairway, and handrails were placed in each bathroom…just in case. There were several additions and alterations like this that Bill Scott came out and did for us during this time. I still could not get used to being unable to use my right hand. I tried to use the hammer, but I couldn't hold the nail. There were several tools and jobs that had to be "adapted" due to my new incapacity.

I was doing quite well with my new routine. My therapy was now just twice each week since the Physical Therapy was an outpatient service now. It started at 9 A.M., so I had to be up and ready because there was a thirty-minute drive up the bay to Mercy Medical in Daphne. Just getting dressed in the morning wouldn't have been so difficult if not for my stubborn nature. I insisted that I could and should get myself dressed to go to therapy each morning. Getting my clothes on took half an hour, but I did it. Dianne was like a patient mother waiting for the kids to get dressed for school in the morning. Every day it was a different struggle because of the different clothes. I found sitting was the answer for me. In Occupational Therapy, they had taught us ways to get in and out of our clothes, but you never go over things like how to button your pants with one hand. I found that if they were a size larger I could pull them together and button them with one hand. All of my clothes were now a size larger anyway since I had lost so much weight through this ordeal.

Tying my shoes presented the biggest challenge each morning, sometimes 10 to 15 minutes for each shoe—try tying a shoelace with one hand! One morning I started getting dressed and I saw these new shoes sitting in my regular shoe spot. I asked Dianne what these were sitting there. She smiled and said, "A new type of shoe that you'll be happy they developed in the last year or so." They were "stringless" athletic shoes—no tying: just slip them on and go; they were great. That shoe technology saved me a great deal of time and aggravation. I became a walking testimonial for them as an aid to a stroke victim. I wanted to call them "Stump shoes," but I thought I'd better not because amputees would misunderstand my meaning.

I began to make strides in my progress at the rehab hospital. For example, I could pedal the hand cycle unit with both hands and then with just the right hand alone. Feeling and movement started to return in my right foot and toes. My walking became better, and I was able to get on the treadmill now and walk a few minutes.

My progress at home was better too. After leaving the inpatient treatment schedule, I began having the acupuncture treatments at home. Acupuncture is not a painful process for the patient; it usually feels about like a hair being pulled from a person's arm and some say, it's like a mosquito bite. You can hardly feel the insertion in most acupuncture cases. In the beginning I was not aware of it at all. Then one day all of a sudden I could feel the sensation that was supposed to be in the arm and wanted to see what the neurologist said at his next examination.

Then I began to feel sensation come back into my toes; I could not determine flexion and extension, but I could determine touch now. I noticed that I could remove my shoes just using my feet as one does when lazy. I was getting out of the house more now, trying to walk. The uneven turf was a real challenge, as was just walking. I fell many times getting the proper balance, and my right knee was very weak and a little painful. I described my problem with the knee pain, acupuncture was done on it for a couple of weeks, and I haven't had the problem since. I've had many other problems, but not the knee weakness and pain.

Balance was the real difficulty because I could hardly feel the right side when I put my foot down to take a step. I began to explore what I could do outside and around the house as well.

Dianne asked me to go to the 401 Professional Centre offices one night while she cleaned. I agreed, but when I got there I found myself getting bored just watching her. I asked if I could try vacuuming. It was something I had seen done in the office for years but had really never taken the time to do myself. It soon became the most important job in the world to me. If I could do this, I could again be useful. It took some effort, but I was finally able to get the job done. The most difficult part was trying to pull the vacuum with one hand because I was still unable to use my right hand, and even though I could walk, I could not move my leg without thinking about the mechanical function as I had done so many times before the stroke.

Every movement required a great deal of effort and at the end of the cleaning I was in a sweat. I now had a whole new respect for Dianne and the others who had cleaned the office for so many years. I had to start at the basics in more ways than I thought.

In May of 2000 (though I was not even aware of what year it was until nearly eight months after the stroke), Dianne had contacted Vocational Rehabilitation Services of Alabama, and they had agreed to pay for my physical therapy at Mercy Medical for two more months. The therapy was different then; there was not so much caring and effort to guide my progress as there had been before. Was it the fact that I was no longer a full-time patient? Still, by the end of June I could see more progress. I could now whistle for the first time since the stroke. Not that they had me work on whistling but I had noticed I could not pucker and use my facial muscles as before, and trying to whistle was good therapy for this. I had always been a great whistler. At one time I could whistle very loudly through my fingers. I could create two separate pitches using only two fingers of the same hand. Then there was the whistle between my thumbs. I could whistle from a very young age. My father had taught me to use different methods of whistling to mean different things when we were in the forest hunting and fishing in case we became separated somehow.

    My progress was good, and my strength was coming back. I was able to handle a wheelbarrow with nearly fifty pounds of "stuff" piled on it. Greg, a painter, another friend and patient, had been working on our downstairs floor at our home and had the debris in bags piled out back. I thought it looked like something I could handle, and I wanted to help clean up around the house since we were thinking about selling the property. I loaded and wheeled the debris to the side of the road for pickup. I was proud that I had accomplished a small feat helping around the house.

    One afternoon a couple of friends called and invited us to go to the "boats" (offshore gambling casinos) in Biloxi. We had gone over there the previous year with Ed and Randa, but I had been in the wheelchair and could not get around. This year I was somewhat ambulatory so we said sure, we would like to go. There were times when I needed some assistance, but as long as we walked slowly, I could get around. I still had to pull down the slot machine handle with the left hand, but I developed a new therapy by placing my right hand on the handle and pushing down with my left hand. I used it to give my right arm exercise but realized this therapy could get almost as expensive as my regular physical therapy had been.

We had a good time and came back with a few quarters in our pockets!

Chapter 7

A New Era

The superior man is distressed by the limitations of his ability; he is not distressed by the fact that men do not recognize the ability he has.
Confucius

Today was the last day of an era of challenge and contentment in my life from the martial arts. It was the day of the closing ceremony of my leadership of the Alabama Shorinji Kempo organization, a role that began in 1986. But, initially started in the fall of 1972 when I struck a deal with Dr. Shingo Fukinbara to teach him English and help him get through Palmer College of Chiropractic in Davenport, Iowa, if he would teach me acupuncture and the martial art of Shorinji Kempo. He had come from Japan and spoke very little English. I was already a black belt in karate but the Kempo looked so smooth and dynamic that I just had to learn the ancient Kung Fu system as well.

Since that period at Palmer College I had been instrumental in setting up Shorinji Kempo schools in Spartanburg, South Carolina; Atlanta, Georgia; and Delmar, Delaware, as well as here in Alabama. Delmar was actually my first location as Branch Master. I had been an assistant to

Dr. Fukinbara since 1972 when we established the Iowa branch.

The Point Clear School in Alabama derived its roots from the old Chinese Shaolin Su Kempo, which was an extension from Kung Fu, somewhere around 5000 years ago. It was systemized and re-named as Shorinji Kempo when taken to Japan. It is now centered in Southern Japan since shortly after World War II. This was historic in itself, but I would have to search the archives to give you the exact details of the transition of martial arts system. This martial art had become a focal point of my nonprofessional life. I had traveled and studied at Hombu, the headquarters in Takamatsu, Japan, studied and talked with the founder and leader, *So Doshin*, several times before his death in 1979. Now, many years had passed, and it was time for others to take over the leadership role. It was time for new ideas and changes. I had selected Richard "Rusty" Loftin as the new Branch Master. He is an attorney and federal prosecutor in Mobile, Alabama by profession, but, more importantly, he understood the "philosophy" of Shorinji Kempo. I believed he would carry on the principles and the philosophy that So Doshin had asked me to take back to the United States and teach to its people after my period of study in Japan years ago.

I had been one of the first Americans to be recognized as a *Jun Kenshi, a Shorinji Kempo black belt,* enrolled through headquarters in 1972. There were a few Americans in Kempo, but they stayed in Japan or were Japanese-American by descent. The difference was, I had studied in America first and became a black belt under Fukinbara sensei in Davenport, Iowa and then went to Japan. There was a school in "Japanese town" in Los Angeles, California, from about 1969, but to my knowledge they did not teach any "round-eye" Americans at that time! The school was run by Sensei Yamamori and still exists today as one of the leading schools of Shorinji Kempo outside of Japan. I loved to travel to Los Angeles and see Yamamori sensei even though at the time I could say only a few words in Japanese. The Doin (temple) there was very authentic, much like you would find in Kyoto, Osaka, or Shikoku, Japan.

    The ceremony took several hours, for I was not in a hurry and knew this would be my last. All the black belts were in the front row, the brown belts in the second row, green belts in the third, and white belts in the last line. They all stood there so proudly as we performed the ceremony. They had done a very commendable job while I was absent that year from the effects of the stroke. Rusty Loftin, my assistant and highest ranking black belt and had taken over like the master he had become. I was very emotional and "full feeling" as I handed out the promotions. Some of the members had been with me nearly 10 years. It felt like sending your children off to college, you know you would never have them there with you like before but you knew they had to go out on their own.

    I had decided to totally hand the leadership over to Rusty. For as long as I was there they would always defer decisions to me out of respect. I wanted Rusty to be able to have total responsibility and control of the Alabama Shorinji Kempo organization and that was the only way for me to accomplish this goal. This organization was not under a democratic system. From the historical perspective it had been patriarchally and dictatorially established and governed from the time So Doshin brought the organization from China to Japan. Even after his daughter Ki So, now the president of the World Shorinji Kempo Organization, took over the organization of several million, primarily men, from all over the globe, it was still governed by her decisions. I wanted Rusty to be able to take control and make the decisions that were expected. Rusty being an attorney by profession had a tendency to be democratic. With me out of the leadership picture he would have to become the decision maker.

A few years earlier I had been one of the front-row black belts in a ceremony in Kyoto, Japan, called a world *taikai*. It was unbelievable to see, let alone to be a part of; six thousand black belts standing in the front and doing a *kata* (a pre-arranged sequence of defensive kick and punch movements) together, all in a sequence not a split-second off. It was like the synchronized sports in the Olympics that I had been involved in during the 1988 Olympic games in Seoul.

In 1998 I had taken five of our black belts from Alabama to Japan to be a part of the unique experience of a taikai. We still talk about the feeling and aura of being in the *budokan* (arena) with thousands of a like mind and *budo* spirit. That night it was all I could do not to shed a tear when each name was called to come forward to receive a certificate or belt. These were my last students after so many superb *kenshi* (students) over the 30 years.

I flashed back on the many trips to Japan, China, India, Europe and South America. I had been helping to promote the Shorinji Kempo legacy and all the comradery and friendship that I had been a part of in this fine organization. To understand and lead in Shorinji Kempo it had to be from a Zen perspective. Not the religious perspective but the spiritual aspect. The heart of the leader had to be directed by Zen spirit but the hand and the fist was to be fast and fearless in its direction to the target. That way you could be any religion and still practice Shorinji Kempo just like you can be any religion and still be an active member of the Rotary International Organization. The same spirit of love and human kindness prevails in all the decisions that are made by these two fine humanitarian administrative bodies.

That evening, I officially stepped down and handed the reigns of leadership over to Rusty. On one hand I was very sad at having to leave and give up something I had cherished so much, but yet I was happy to see that we had planted the seed of this organization and it had grown so well here in Alabama. I had many to thank for this help, and especially Tracey and Walter who had been my dojo assistants in Delaware and then Tracey took over the Delmarva Shorinji Kempo School when I moved to Alabama and here he was in Alabama helping me again.

We had even opened up several other branches in Alabama, like Birmingham and Huntsville. They were being run by some of our best black belts. Dr. Todd in our Birmingham branch was one of them and was especially tuned into the philosophical and spiritual leadership of Shorinji Kempo, and when love and marriage took him from the Eastern Shore of Alabama area we felt this was the right time to start another branch. Big Craig will more than likely get his third degree black belt soon and open another branch here in Alabama.

It was just a part of that yin/yang world relationship that one must deal with in life. Where you see the change from daylight to darkness and then from darkness to daylight and know that this is the true way of nature. I had always found Shorinji Kempo very centering for my life, and I was sure that Rusty would lead the Alabama school in the same direction. I had tried to plant the basic philosophical principles in their mind as Dr. Fukinbara and So Doshin had mine so many years ago and I was sure this would continue with this leadership change.

Dr. John L. Stump

Chapter 8

Lame Dancer

*Some people march to a different drummer –
and some dance.*
John L. Stump

Later in June of that same year 2000, Dianne and I went to the Grand Summer Ball held by Thomas Hospital in Fairhope, the same hospital that had saved my life earlier that year. We had a full table, and everyone had a great time. After a short award presentation to our friend Dr. Betty Ruth Speir, a Fairhope gynecologist, for her many long years as an outstanding doctor to the community, a wonderful meal was served. How did I dance at this ball?

At one time I had been a pretty good dancer. I was even voted "Best Dancer" in my high school, North Caroline, in Denton, Maryland, and at several Buddy Dean Hops around the Baltimore – Washington area. I tried to do some of the moves as well as possible, but for the most part I knew I could only stand and gyrate to the music. Actually, I "did great," Dianne said. I couldn't move around much, and I had to slide my right leg because it was still like a piece of concrete. Dianne really knew I had her in a loving grip because the spasticity seemed worse when I was tense, and I unconsciously pulled her very tightly to me. We stayed up until 12:30 A.M. for the first time since the stroke had attacked me.

The next day Dianne had a bad stomach ache—too much weekend? I told her not to bother to get up and take me to Mercy Medical Hospital in Daphne for my physical therapy as she had done countless times before. This time I was going to do it myself. I got a shower and got dressed (all by myself) and went down and got in my little GMC pickup truck and was off to Mercy Medical, about twenty-five miles on busy Highway 98. I had no problems going, and the therapy was practically uneventful that day.

After therapy, it was back to Fairhope. I came by way of Scenic 98, which was a little slower but a more scenic route on the East side of Mobile Bay. The only problem was the schools were letting out. I went slowly through Daphne and beautiful Montrose, but coming into Fairhope I looked down and noticed I needed gas. The station where we buy gas is near our old office, on the way into Fairhope. So I pulled in to fill up.

It was very busy and I was very slow. However, I filled up and decided to pull up out of the way so others could get gas. The station is on a slight hill; for most people it is nothing, but for me it was a challenge! Up the hill and into the gas station I moved like a snail I know. I paid for the gas and chatted with Mark, the owner, for a minute, but he was very busy and I soon said good-bye. Coming out of the door there was a very high step and no handrail. That presented a problem. I had learned that if I turned slightly to right and stepped off with my strong side, then brought my weak side down, it was easier, but as I was trying to negotiate the movements necessary someone opened the door, I lost my balance and down I went.

I tried to get up quickly so no one would see me. That was impossible, of course; getting up from a fall or a prone position is very hard. I knew I could get up, but between trying to tell everyone I was not hurt and trying to get up there was a real scene. Several people wanted to pull me to my feet, but I asked them not to. I wanted to get up myself by rolling onto my strong side, which is my left, pushing up to my elbow, then to a sitting position; from there I could come to my knees and then up to a standing position. This took some time, and I'm sure it was a real show, but I was determined to get up on my own.

Suppose I had fallen in a location where there was no one to help, was I to lie there and yell for help? No, if I wasn't hurt I would get up on my own! This I finally accomplished after some maneuvering to get in the proper position.

Down the hill and back to the truck was the next item on the agenda. I was standing and had reassured everyone I was fine, except for the embarrassment. I had never walked up or downhill without some assistance; today was going to be the day, I thought. I found that walking on a level surface was fine, but when that surface began to change slope, the propreoceptive mechanism in my joints and muscles was not functioning normally. I could not tell when my right foot touched the ground except when my leg stopped moving. I slowly walked down the hill to the truck and found it was easier to go up than come down an incline. I should have known this from going up and down the steps at home but I guess that had also slipped through the cracks. Then there was getting in and getting the truck started, but that was not a problem after what I had just accomplished getting gas.

Off I went through the middle of town at the busy time of day. Then I thought, since I was doing so well, maybe I would look at a few houses on the way home, which was a bit of a challenge. I did manage to look at about three houses that were for sale on the way home. I knew I wouldn't tell Dianne about the little fall. She would worry that I couldn't do anything on my own without having an accident or needing assistance.

I glanced at my watch and noticed that it was 4:30 P.M., and we were usually home by then if we hadn't stopped at the store for milk or something. I figured I better get on down the bay. It had clouded up and now it started to rain very hard, as is so common in Alabama. I was less than five minutes away from home when the rain stopped. A few more minutes, and there it was…home—Quietwater, as we had named it the week we moved in nearly fifteen years ago.

I pulled the truck into its regular parking spot, got out and headed for the steps. I was still having a real problem getting up and down the steps, there were just so many to negotiate. The yard was very spacious, with a great variety of shrubs and trees, an addition to our home built a few years prior by a retired CIA agent and his wife who had spent 10 years in China during the Shagkishek break from Mainland China. Another story I would like to tell some day. There was also a guest house, pool, pier, pier house, and bulkhead on the property to maintain. Needless to say, Dianne and I had decided to sell since I couldn't keep all this up anymore in my condition. It was beautiful, but just too much for me (us) to maintain now. I had liked doing a lot of the work around the house, yard and boathouse before my stroke, but now I could do nothing. A place on Mobile Bay like ours required constant work to keep up. It was like living on a ranch…always a fence to mend.

I really felt good with the exception of a few bruises and a damaged ego from the fall. I had driven myself to therapy and back. By the time I arrived home, Dianne was now up and feeling better. She said that getting up and having breakfast had helped a great deal. So I told her that we would have to make dancing a part of my therapy and go out now and then to see my progress. This suggestion she seemed to like.

Looking back on the Thomas Hospital benefit ball made me realize just how much our life was like a dance. One minute you are going forward, then all of a sudden you are turned around going backward, then it's a total spin, over and over again and all to the rhythm and music of life!

I do want to emphasize just how important exercise is when you've had a stroke. Getting strength, balance and your total daily endurance back to as good as possible is primary on every person's mind. To be able to do this with something as enjoyable as dancing is a real treat. It not only helps all the physical infirmities but it is a wonderful way to keep your mind and emotions on an even temperament. I thought of how nice it would be if my friend Susie who teaches dancing could have a class at the rehab hospital teaching the stroke patients dancing. This would make the entire process of therapy a lot more bearable for most.

Dr. John L. Stump

Chapter 9

Return to Teaching

*To be helped after a stroke, you must agree to be taught
t many things which you already know.*
John L. Stump

September 2001 marked another point in my progress. I wanted to return to teaching at the Alabama Oriental Studies Institute (AOSI), a private school of higher education, which Dianne and I founded in Point Clear, Alabama, about 10 years earlier. This school had allowed us to teach the many different aspects of Oriental culture that had been missing from the southern Alabama area where I lived until the Institute became a reality in 1989.

My acupuncture class usually had about 15 people and was formed to teach martial arts students as well as laypeople about the principles of Oriental medicine. I had taught this acupuncture class for the past ten years here at the Institute. However, I was apprehensive at this time. Would I be able to do it? Would I be able to pronounce the Japanese and Chinese names and enunciate the terms properly for the students? Dianne pushed me to give it a try; after all, I was continuing to do very well with my diction and speech.

My emotional and speech progress was great, the students reported. The class went well with relatively few problems. "It seemed like old times," Rusty, the new Alabama Branch Master commented after the first class. It had been a year since the last class. I was doing a good job with my enunciation and speech as well as, being able to stand in front of the class during the entire session, they remarked. I couldn't believe I was actually back in front of the students answering questions and teaching Oriental philosophy again. This had been my real interest since first becoming acquainted with the subject with Dr. Fukinbara in Japan and continued as I became involved at the University in Shiannx, China. I had become so engrossed in Oriental philosophy that I ended up doing an Oriental Medicine doctoral dissertation for a PhD on "The Theory of Yin and Yang in Oriental Medicine as it Relates to Human Health and Healing."

Shiannx, China, was a very interesting area to live at the time. It is in the western central part of China where the ancient clay statues were such an archeological find. I got a chance to go to several Buddhist museums that were thousands of years old. One museum had stone tablets with writings of the ancient Chinese philosopher *Lutz Su* carved into them. The language on the tablets was so old that only a handful of people had the ability to read them. I also visited the famous Shaolin Temple located not far from Shiannx. This temple became very famous as the martial arts center of the world during the years when the TV series *Kung Fu* was running. It was one of the most famous Buddhist temples in all of China for teaching something most Buddhists are not known for and that was self-defense. The monks there were known as the "fighting monks." They had developed their own method and style of defense that is still taught today. The system I had learned in Japan from Fukinbara sensei and So Doshin and all the teachers at Hombu, called *Shorinji Kempo*, was a system that had its lineage from this famous Buddhist temple.

Shorinji Kempo had become very interesting to me because it taught acupuncture and Zen philosophy as a part of the martial art system. I was very impressed with the philosophy of the *koans* we had to learn. They were little verses that we had to remember and live by to stimulate our thinking, like "Live half for yourself and half for others." At first I didn't know what to think of this philosophical change. Were the Buddhists saying live for yourself first, when we had always in the Christian tradition been taught always serve others first? It took me a little while to understand this. They were teaching that if you serve yourself first to keep strong you would help others more than you could if you served them first and had nothing left over for yourself. This is a simplistic explanation but the essence of some of the 'Koans' and the teaching.

On the physical plane, points on the body are used to stimulate energy and others were used to sedate energy. One could use the sedative points to very effectively defeat an aggressor. Other points were used to stimulate the energy of another person to improve their health, vitality and longevity. This had been a part of the monks teaching system for thousands of years.

Many Chinese historians and authorities believe this is where the ancient art of acupuncture was developed. Shiannx was an old capital city of China, and I could have spent years there, but I had to return to the states. After all my family and earning a living were also important. I had spent much too long on this learning pilgrimage in the Orient many thought.

I was very pleased that I had been able to hold up my end of the bargain by teaching acupuncture at the Institute in Point Clear. No one knew how hard it had been for me to face all those people, college professors, doctors, lawyers and school teachers and not know whether the knowledge would come out in an intelligible manner. I had lost all of the Chinese, Japanese, and Korean and most of the English I had known due to the stroke. But, I was convinced I had to try, and sure enough, it began to return. Now, five years has passed, I have gotten back my English, a great deal of my Japanese, some of my Korean, and a little of the Chinese language skills I once possessed.

A few months ago, I was asked by our Fairhope Rotary president to give the prayer in Japanese because the International world meeting was to be held in Kyoto, Japan. Well, I was not sure that I had regained command enough of the Japanese language to give the prayer. I hesitatingly agreed to give it a go the next week. Low and behold, when I opened my mouth and began to give the prayer it came out just about as perfect as it had years ago.

A few years ago, a neurologist explained the language loss was due to the damage from the bleed in the Broca's area of the brain; he said the languages would return a little at a time over the next several years. He was correct in his explanation, but it has taken the best part of five years for this process of recovery to return in this area.

What I am wondering now is whether I will recover any more from the damage. A 95-year-old patient once told me that he had had a bad stroke when he was about 65 and could not walk or talk for over a year, yet he regained about 75% of his physical capabilities over a 10-year period. I know each stroke is unique, but I would like to assume my progress would be as good as what he described. I know that I will never discourage a friend or patient by telling them they will have very little if any progress after the first six months of a stroke…because it is just not true.

Chapter 10

Personal Therapy

Words of comfort, skillfully administered, are the oldest therapy known to man.
Louise Nizer

For several years now, I have had a personal therapy program underway I need to talk about. I had discussed some of the physical problems I was still having with Evan Grant, a therapist who had worked at my office in Fairhope for about five years. Evan was very intelligent and had an excellent work ethic. He had graduated from Johns Hopkins University several years back, and I was trying to get him motivated to go on into a healthcare specialty—osteopathy, chiropractic, or medicine. His father had been a physician and I could see Evan as a caring doctor. That's why I kept on him about going to school.

One day when we were talking, I mentioned to Evan that I was no longer going to physical therapy because the insurance coverage had run out. He also felt it was certainly bureaucratic the way insurance worked. It covered me while I was at the hospital and now that I was out and doing better, there was no coverage at a time when I had the energy to work at improving even more.

He urged me to set a physical goal each month and work on it each day. He said he had known someone who had suffered a stroke, and this was one of his rehabilitative methods.

These were some of the goals I worked on during that time:

September Turning on the light switch with my right hand.
October Feeding our cat "Whiskers" with my right hand from the Deli-cat jug, a brand that she really liked at that time.
November Shaking hands with people using my right hand.
December Turning the doorknob with my right hand.
January Using both hands when driving.

I still use some of Evan's suggestions to this day. (By the way, he is now a graduate of the medical school of the University of Alabama at Birmingham.) Dianne and I had dinner with Evan and his wife Dawn in Birmingham after a seminar I was teaching on Laser Therapy.

I made driving a part of my personal therapy. Steering with both hands, lifting the right leg, and pushing on the accelerator with my right foot were the most difficult parts, for I still had very little feeling in the lower right leg and foot.

I was going to get a special handicapped rating on my Drivers license that had been arranged through Vocational Rehabilitation Services of Alabama. This would be helpful for my insurance rates and prove there was no detriment in driving. Penny Krigler, my vocational counselor, had arranged for me to take the test that week.

I had been a very good driver before the stroke and even drove an 18 - wheeler (truck) one summer while I was in college. I had no reason to doubt my ability since the stroke. I knew my right arm still didn't function normally and my right leg was a little slow, but hell! I had seen people drive with only one arm, one eye, one leg, no legs, and actually I saw a young man on TV who was able to drive with only his feet, so why couldn't I?

There was no reason to be worried that this test would present any problem. Man, was I wrong! From the very first part to the very last part (actual driving on the road) I felt like they were looking for ways not to pass me. If the tests they put me through were the ones they put every driver through there would be safer drivers or at least more knowledgeable drivers on the road today. They even had me take a reaction time test and a computerized situation test and several other tests I didn't have to take even when I drove the 18-wheeler. Well, I passed the four-hour test with better than 90% score, much to my surprise.

Driving seems to really help my coordination, especially the hand-eye coordination. I never realized the total body functions of the act of driving before the stroke. This was just another function I took for granted in my daily life before the stroke. You can bet I sure respect the operation of a motor vehicle a great deal more today than before the stroke. I still don't venture onto the interstates and freeways because of the oath I took to be a defensive driver, I still do not feel comfortable at 70 miles per hour with two hands, let alone just one.

Another personal therapy I incorporated into my rehab program was aquatic exercise. The physical therapist at Mercy Medical told me the aquatic program at several of the town pools would be very helpful. Of course we had the problem at the time of living so far out of town.

I came home one day and told Dianne that I was going to try the aquatic exercises they had recommended at Mercy Medical using our home pool. My first problem when beginning my new program was getting in the pool. We had a handrail in the pool but there were no steps into and out of the pool, so I could not support myself up and out or into the two feet of water required with my one good hand.

I came to the conclusion I would need help. I called on two of my golfing buddies, Ed Fitzgerald and Mike Moore, one day and asked if they could help me build a ramp or steps down in the pool. They were both handy with building tools and readily agreed they could get the task accomplished.

They were at the house at 8 AM the next Saturday morning and started working. That evening I was up on the platform ready to try it out. They were hot from working all day and said they would help me. I agreed I needed all the help I could get at this point.

I had been a good swimmer in the past and was really into aquatic activity: scuba driving, parasailing, canoeing and sailing, almost anything in or on the water. Here I was getting ready to take a plunge I was really unsure of...but I had to do it if it would help.

Mike and Ed both got in the water and I walked down the well-made sturdy, wooden ramp and the handrail they had made was just the right height. I was like a kid with a new bike...excited but apprehensive. I finally made it down the steps and into the water at the shallow end of the pool. Mike got on one side and Ed on the other and they walked in the water with me for about 10 minutes before they let go. Then it was time to try on my own. This was a strange experience I thought. It felt like I was a beginning astronaut trying to keep my balance. I could not feel my right leg and if I lifted my leg very much it seemed like it would begin to float outward from my body. I kept walking up and down and side-to-side until Mike and Ed were satisfied that I could control myself in the water.

It was getting late and they said they had to go but they wanted to be sure I could also get out of the pool. This I was able to accomplish without any problem because it was like going up the steps at the house. It seemed as though my balance improved dramatically when I had something to touch or to hold; and the handrail they had made was excellent. This is still the case today. Even though I can now walk without a cane I still have trouble with steps that don't have handrails. Just being able to hold something like a handrail causes a remarkable improvement in the balance of the stroke victim. This is because of the propreoceptive (the sensory end organs in the muscles, tendons, etc. that are sensitive to the stimuli originating in these tissues by the movement of the body) mechanism in the body has been damaged due to the effects stroke.

    I went into the house after they had gone to tell Dianne about my new program and how it had felt. I didn't realize it but Dianne had been watching from the window off and on all day. She said she was really impressed at my accomplishment after she had gotten over the laughter from watching me trying to keep my balance in the pool. I laughed with her because I know it looked funny but it was difficult at first.

    As time went on I became more accustomed to the feeling in the water and began to swim both under water and on top. My swimming stroke had to be adapted because I still couldn't get my arm to come forward in the crawl method and my leg was slow; but I could swim!

    I have continued to try to pursue many of these stroke rehabilitative practices even though I have been released from any care except my own. I will continue to work just as hard as I did in the beginning to try to overcome the detriments to my body and brain. Even though many experts say that this is not possible, I want to continue just in case they happen to be wrong and they have been known to be wrong at times in the past! For I was not supposed to be able to walk or talk again, but I am now doing all the tasks they said I wouldn't be able to do. So, you see, that is why I don't just take even the experts' word. I want it proven to me!

Chapter 11

To Sell or Not to Sell...that is the Question

Opportunities are often things you haven't noticed the first time around.
Catherine Deneuve

The year 2000 proved to be a difficult year due to the many decisions I had to face. I had put our house on the market several months earlier. At the time, I really didn't think about it, but now we had an offer. Would we be better in the long run, selling or staying? This decision was now facing us for real, and we had to make a decision. This was the third offer we had and the best to date. It was very close to our asking price and they wanted it immediately.

Dianne and I left for a mini-vacation at Lake Martin, in the foothills of the Appalachian Mountains in northern Alabama, to think about what we were going to do. I drove for the first time on the interstate since my stroke, but there were no problems. We stopped in Montgomery and had sushi and sashimi for lunch at a nice little Japanese spot along I-85 that had recently opened. Then it was back on the road until we got to the lake, where we have a timeshare that we had not been able to use for the past two years due to all the lecturing commitments and the stroke. The time at the lake was good. We went for long, slow walks, sat by the lake, and had a relaxed week. I doubled my walking distance that week, and we made the important decision about the house.

Upon our return, the first thing we had to face was my full release from Mercy Medical Hospital. I had made good progress while in rehabilitation. I was happy because I had accomplished much that many, including myself, had thought I would never be able to accomplish. I was sad because my progress was slowing now to the point that it had been very negligible for the last couple of months. I guess I had known in the back of my mind that this day would come and my progress would slow or even eventually stop by any conventional measure. This I really do not admit but can understand from a doctor's perspective. The burden of the remainder of the therapy or improvement was now on me. This I accepted and will go on one day at a time but always forward.

The next thing was the sale of the house. We had selected another house in the city of Fairhope, a one-story brick with smaller yard and no pool, as low-maintenance as possible. We actually at that time lived in the town of Point Clear, a small area a few miles southeast of Fairhope. We made the move with the help of a lot of our friends. The Boston Whaler, the Yukon SUV, diving gear, fishing gear, camping and hiking gear were all sold or given away because I knew they could never be used again. What about my guns and bows? I had loved longbow hunting but was now pretty sure I would never be able to shoot again. I decided to give this equipment to my family members. Almost all of them like to hunt and fish, so they would put the prized equipment to good use. That night I called my brother Doug who lived in Delaware and told him of my decision. We would bring the things up when I came to see Mom that summer.

Scuba diving

I told Mike Lipscomb, a diver and one of my kempo black belt instructors, to take the scuba gear that I didn't think I would be using again, everything from tanks to dive charts. Some of the equipment was new, some years old, for as I remember, it was 1968–69 that I started diving on the shores of Rehoboth Beach and Ocean City, on the Delmarva Peninsula. As a University of Maryland student I became interested in the Chesapeake Bay and surrounding waters and took my first scuba diving class. As I looked back at the logbooks I realized that it had been more than thirty years since the beginning class in diving, and it had taken me all over the world for the sport and pleasure of it. I had traveled to Hawaii, the Caribbean and Virgin Islands, Haiti, Dominican Republic, Alaska, Tahiti, Australia's great barrier reef, and many other interesting places.

But now I was closing that chapter of my life. No longer could I lift a tank, or the weight belt for that matter, without great difficulty. I could not even stand up on my boat or any other dive boat for that matter. I did enjoy the undersea life, the quiet solitude of diving; it was sure a different world under the ocean. I had valued and experienced about every type of diving the amateur could. I even joined a treasure diving group in Delaware when Mel Fisher and his group were investing millions in the treasure hunting market. We found a few gold chains, bars, artifacts, but about that time I got involved with the Olympic games and diving took a back seat.

Then I noticed that emotion was about to overcome me in this process of reminiscence. Would I ever be good enough to do anything constructive again for work or pleasure? As I went through the diving equipment with Mike I remembered many stories that went with each piece of equipment. Swimming had proved difficult enough in the past months. I loved the water and it was hard to admit that I wouldn't be able to participate in the activities I had in the past. Most people my age had given up water sports and diving long ago. However, there were a few diehards like me who were hanging on as long as possible. Besides our son Mike was an avid scuba diver and might be willing to let me go out with him sometime in the future.

For the next week, if it hadn't been for several of my black belts like 'big Craig' coming to help move us I don't think that we could have gotten everything done in time. Craig is extremely big and strong and could carry the heavy concrete tables and benches that we had in the yard. We had selected the concrete because the high winds on the bay would come up quickly and blow everything else into the water. Craig would just take the parts that it would take two men to carry and stick them under each arm and load them onto the truck. The other kempo guys that helped me, Earl, Art, Rusty and Mike were all impressed that day with Craig's incredible strength.

Over the next week or so Dianne, Ed, Randa, Mike and Sue got our household items moved into our new house in Fairhope. The new location was about a mile off the bay in town. Convenient to all the locations it had taken so long to drive to before the stroke. Again, Dianne had seen the need for locating us closer to the facilities we may need in the future, hospital, doctors, pharmacies, stores, etc. It's just a fact that I didn't want to face. Being down in the 'boon-docks' in outer Point Clear on a little spit on land between Weeks Bay and Mobile Bay was what I had liked. But, just like the night of my stroke it took them a good 20 minutes to get down to the house and another 10 minutes to get me loaded and 20 minutes or more to the hospital. That's a lot of time to pass when someone is having a stroke. Dianne wanted to be closer if something else did happen, because the doctors said this would probably be the case.

Getting the person who may be in need of medical attention to the proper facility as soon as possible may mean all the difference in the recovery of that person from the stroke effects. This is why the move became a priority once I gained more cognitive ability and understood the worry this would take off Dianne.

Chapter 12

A New Millennium

The time is always right to do what is right.
Rev. Martin Luther King

The beginning of a new millennium introduced a new chapter not only of this book but of my life as well. Changes and progress were still being made, but very slowly. Evan Grant, my physical therapist, had said he could still see improvement in the strength in my right hamstring muscle when he did the therapy on my legs and feet, as well as the range-of-motion exercises we did twice each week. Also, I had continued my acupuncture. I noticed more progress in my hand movement. This movement was different because it was what had been absent in my muscular movement for the past four months—extension! The movements of the body are described in specific terms of medical terminology in this regard. Most everyone understands flexion because most all of our movements during our waking hours are flexion movements. The opposite movement of flexion of a body part is call extension. For example when you make a fist this is called flexion of the fingers. Then when you open the hand it is called extension of the fingers.

For all these months I had good—well, pretty good—contraction but no extension. Today after the treatment with

Evan there was extension of each finger. That extension was weak, but present. Now again, I had something to work toward!

That afternoon Dianne came in the house with a sad look on her face, a look I was not used to seeing, as she was always good at concealing her emotions. She would have been a good poker player. She sat down and a tear came to her eye as she started to speak. "Today, I got a call from the doctor who did the MRI and CAT scans Monday," she said. I had been examined every two or three weeks since I was released from Mercy Medical. It had been nearly four months since my stroke, and they were trying to find out why I had it in the first place. I guess the priority had been to save my life, then to see if I was going to live, and now they were interested to determine what had been the culprit.

"The doctor said that you need to come back tomorrow," Dianne went on. "They see something on the scan and want to make sure. They will do another scan tomorrow. He said they think they see a tumor on your adrenal or kidney area. The doctor's are not certain, John. What does this mean?"

"Well, I'm not sure except that they want to be sure before they say."

"A tumor—does this mean cancer?"

"Not always," I assured her. "There are benign tumors that are not cancerous. Let's wait and see what the scan shows tomorrow."

The next morning we were there at 8 A.M. I was anxious to see what had taken me down so easily—no symptoms, no pain, nothing. I was in perfect health, I thought! I had not gotten much sleep the night before, trying to figure out what it was we were looking for, and neither had Dianne. She was restless, but for other reasons, I imagined. Was she soon to be a widow? Was I eaten up with cancer? I had heard horror stories all through school of patients going right up to the last few months not knowing they had a mass or tumor. Was I to be one of those statistics?

Pheochromocytoma...what Is It?

Pheochromocytoma was the diagnosis for now, a tumor of the adrenal gland. I had more full body scans, MRIs, CAT scans, blood and urine tests and every other test to confirm the diagnosis. They still would not know whether it was a cancerous or benign tumor until they did the surgery and a biopsy once it was removed. It seemed as though there was no choice but to remove the tumor. Radiation and chemotherapy had not proven beneficial with this type of tumor the doctors had told Dianne. The trouble was this was a very rare tumor, and very few surgeons had ever removed one. A few years ago this would have been a death sentence.

The doctors' vote was to send me to MD Anderson, a hospital in Houston, Texas named for Monroe Anderson, with a sterling reputation for cancer research and tumors of rare origin like mine. At MD Anderson the surgeons had a great deal of experience with this type of tumor and performed procedures on many patients from all over the world. My first inclination was to go with what had been suggested and arrangements were made. Then that evening a strange feeling came over me, a reluctant feeling. I didn't say anything right away; I wanted to wait. This was a big decision I had to make, another life-and-death choice? I told Dianne I wanted to talk to Dr. Dan Stubler, my neurologist and one of the doctors responsible for suspecting the pheochromocytoma. Dr. Kimerly, an endocrinologist, had been the one who actually made the diagnosis. But Dr. Stubler had the suspicion and had referred me to Dr. Kimerly to confirm the diagnosis. We scheduled an appointment for the consultation. I felt very comfortable with Dr. Stubler; he had been my neurologist at Mercy Medical and had continued seeing me when I was released to outpatient status.

I told Dr. Stubler I had some reservations about going to Houston. I knew that was where I would get top-rate care, but I did not want to put my wife and family through the difficulties of dealing with new doctors, staff, and strange location in a distant city if we didn't have to. Couldn't the surgery be done in Mobile or Birmingham? I asked. He said he understood and questioned if I could give him a day or two to see if there was anyone in the area who could do the procedure.

In two days we got a call from Dr. Stubler. There was a Dr. Davidson who had just been transferred to a hospital in Mobile from MD Anderson Hospital in Houston that had performed all the procedures we had been talking about. Dr. Stubler asked us to set up a consult with Dr. Davidson. Dr. Davidson's office quickly set up an appointment for us to discuss the surgical procedure with him that week.

The doctor was young, in his mid-forties, and well spoken. He explained the procedure and all of its details. He also stated that he had done five of the operations with no complications. They were risky, and he could not guarantee that I would not lose my kidney in the process; half of the others had. The worst thing about a 'pheo' he said was the unpredictability, that was the reason the mortality with this surgery was so high.

I was satisfied with the answers he had given and told him we would call the next day with our decision. My dad had always told me to sleep on a big decision and the answer would be clearer the next day. That was my intention. Dianne and I went home and began to make plans. If the procedure was successful and the tumor was benign, we would do one thing, and well, if it were cancerous, we would have another decision to make. She didn't want to think about it, but I said we had to make plans in case the procedure was a failure and I didn't make it off the table. Also, if the tumor was cancerous, what were the options? I wanted to go ahead with the procedure at the Mobile Infirmary with Dr. Davidson.

The next morning Dianne called his office and told him we wanted to schedule the surgery as soon as possible here in Mobile. The procedure was scheduled for later the same week. For some reason I felt a strange calm for the next few days. Dianne, on the other hand, was as jumpy as the proverbial "cat on a hot tin roof." Plans were made, changed, made again, and a million *"what if*s" came to mind. Finally the day arrived. There was no more delay; I was checking into the hospital that morning.

I was again put through a series of scans—I guess to confirm the location of the tumor—then scheduled for the surgical procedure to begin the next morning at 8 A.M. Dianne stayed with me at the hospital that night. We talked late into the night, after all I didn't know if it would be my last chance to spend a few quality hours alone with the woman I loved so much. The next morning I remember going down to the surgical area for an injection, kissing Dianne, and then I was out before I could count backward from a hundred.

I didn't wake for eight hours they tell me. They had removed the tumor and my right adrenal gland. The surgeon had saved the right kidney but they had to remove my left kidney and the other major organs in the abdominal area to do an exploratory procedure in case there was more of the tumor to be found. I had an incision from the left side to the right that followed the bottom of my rib cage all the way across my abdominal area.

I will have to say recovering from this surgery was one of the most difficult ordeals I have ever had to endure. I was so swollen from the medications and the surgery that it took several months before I could move about at all. Again I pulled through and the tumor was found to be benign, so there was good news in this story. There were several more months of rehabilitation to go through just to get back to where I had been before the surgery. Here I was, nearly six months after the stroke, just beginning my climb back up the mountain again. Just like the old school days, just about the time you are at the top you're knocked back down the hill again. But, I was determined to crawl back to the top again and again if I had to. Dr. Fukinbara had said many years ago that *tenacity* was one of my traits and that's something you must develop after surviving a stroke. Don't give up on a task; keep at it like it's your last chance!

When I talked with a neurologist in the hospital where I had the surgery about my pheochromocytoma, he said that it was an adrenal tumor and he didn't know what caused it since I didn't have any of the typical symptoms associated with the tumor: severe headache, palpitations, rapid heart rate, sweating, flushing, chest pain, abdominal pain, nervousness, irritability, increased appetite, loss of weight, hand tremor and or high blood pressure. I did have one symptom but I had this difficulty since high school and that was "sleeping difficulty." I rarely slept more than four hours each night. I never felt bad and it didn't seem to bother me. I just thought I was one of those people who didn't require much sleep.

For patients who have non-cancerous tumors surgically removed, the 5-year survival rate was 95% Dianne found out from the surgeon, with recurrence in less than 10% of patients. So, my odds seemed pretty good to survive this problem, at least for now.

In a few weeks Dianne was back on the phone to Alabama Department of Rehabilitation explaining my ordeal, to see if more therapy could be worked out. Penny Kruger, my rehabilitation advisor had somehow made arrangements for another month of therapy. She had been great to do what she had through Alabama Rehabilitation services but we knew the compensation was running thin.

Several weeks went by before I could move because of the edema. My entire body felt like an over-inflated beach ball. But, soon I was back at Mercy Medical doing my old therapy routine again. I still had to be careful because the incision site was still weak. The incision looked like I had done *hara-kiri* or at least tried - this is where the Japanese people would cut all the way across the abdominal section to commit suicide - with a scar going from my right kidney across my abdomen to my left kidney, and at times it felt like I had. The incision followed my rib cage all the way from the left side of the body to the right side. I had tried to joke with the surgeon about putting in a zipper in case they had to open me up again. Of course he didn't think it was funny, nor for that matter did most of the people that I told. Within the next month or two the incision was pretty strong and my therapy started having better results the doctors felt.

Of course I felt as though I had been put back to square one in this whole ordeal. I knew I had to look at it from the positive side. At least they found the tumor that originally caused the stroke, had removed it, and determined it was benign. Now, I had to return to the physical and mental point of getting back into the game. I thought to myself many times that I may just have to give up, it was just too hard, the road to recovery was so long. But, I couldn't, I had never given up on anything. I had been knocked down the hill again, but I was going to get up and keep climbing until I was back on top again!

Chapter 13

Back on the Road Again

The great thing in this world is not so much where we stand as in what direction we are moving.
Oliver Wendell Holmes, Sr.

During the first year and most of the second year after my stroke, I felt as though there was another person possessing my body. Especially when I could not walk, talk or remember anything from my short-term or long-term memory. My mind seemed to be like a sieve instead of the sponge it used to be.

My normal feeling gradually returned over this two-year period and I could now say that I felt 80 % the same as before the stroke. I'm not sure what to call this feeling except a presence. I did not feel that I was in possession or control of my body before this time, and I guess I wasn't. I knew there were still physical impairments that had to be reconciled, but I was also aware of the improvements in my emotional and mental state in the past two years. I seemed to make great leaps forward emotionally at this time, and I was like Rip Van Winkle just waking up from a dream. I realize now it was no dream…rather a nightmare.

With my mental clarity and feeling back to normal, I had regained, at least partially, my physical capacity and all but my language ability. The neurologist, Dr. Stubler, said the damage in those areas of my brain that control the languages might be years in returning. I could live without speaking Japanese, Chinese and the others; I was just happy to be speaking English again!

Even now after five years there is still a heavy weakness on the right side of my body and uncoordinated loss of muscular power in much of my movement, which I hope I can continue to get control of as time goes along. I have been working out at a local wellness center for the past couple of years and that has helped with my coordination and strength.

I can tell from the numbers that I am getting back much of my strength. When I started two years ago, I could not get on the treadmill: the speed could not be calibrated low enough for me to walk. After six months of working out, I could get on the treadmill at the level of one mile per hour for three minutes. I can now do two miles per hour for 25 minutes. When I began, I could not do a single, complete sit-up; after one year I could do 50 and then a100 sit-ups. I am up to 200 and try to add 100 sit-ups per year. At one time I could whip off 500 sit-ups or push-ups without a second thought. I want to thank Trish for all her help and assistance as a wonderful caring Personal Trainer during those early years of my personal rehabilitation at the Wellness Center.

The resistance machines also tell a tale of my progress; for example, when I started the leg press, I could do only 75 pounds; now I am up over 200 pounds. My workout routine on Mondays, Wednesdays, and Fridays includes 10 or more of these machines. The whole routine takes me about 90 minutes and sometimes longer (depending on how much I talk when I should be working).

I have noticed very little improvement in the heaviness, muscular control and coordination returning to my arm or my leg in the past year or so. There still remains a numb sensation on the right side of my body. I can tell when I shave that the left side of my face feels normal while the right is about 50% less than the normal feel. Will this sensation become normal after more time? Everyone's progress is a little different. Mine got better over two or three years but I would have to say there is a way to go to get back to 'normal.'

On the other hand, my cognition, mental, and emotional gains have been significant in the past couple of years. My ability to speak returned six months after the stroke and I wanted to do everything possible to reinforce this progress. I practiced talking with marbles in my mouth. I began with two and went up to five. I repeated the alphabet forward and backward three times each day. I really worked hard at regaining my language ability even by trying to sing which I never could do! I wanted to get my communication skills back more than anything. But even after I found that I was able to talk, the processing of the words was not there and only came a little at a time over the next year. For instance I would be trying to carry on a conversation and I would find that a word that I was thinking I wanted to say just would not come out of my mouth. I would then have to search my mind for one that could be processed and my mouth and lips could utter. It was very strange but I had to keep at it and I just knew the language skills would get better with use.

After thinking about what I could do to help myself I then decided that a computer would help me with cognitive function. After talking to several of my friends who had computers, I decided on a laptop. I always had computers in my office since 1972, when I bought one the size of a small submarine. It took two people six months to input the data, and by the time they had finished the project, small personal computers were on the market for half the price. I tried for the next several years to keep up with the technology but progress was happening too fast, unless you were in that field, to keep up. For the next 25 years I hired employees who were computer literate to do the office stats and accounting.

I had to laugh; it was a new millennium, and I was just starting to learn the hardware and software technology again. I no longer had an office full of secretaries I could ask to do the work. I was alone now with one usable hand and arm for the keyboard. Could I do it? Was I up to the challenge? You're reading the result. I know my copy editors have done an awful lot to help me get this manuscript to a readable format. However, I was determined to get it done and out so the public could read my story and how to possibly prevent a stroke in their life or the life someone close to them.

Lake Martin Escape

Just a year before I had the stroke Dianne and I had bought a timeshare at beautiful Lake Martin in Northwest Alabama in the foothills of the Appalachian Mountains. Here there was a golf course (part of the Robert Trent Jones Golf Trail), which I thought was great. I had just returned to playing Golf in the past few years with Ed, Mike and some of the guys at the Quail Creek golf course. In addition to the golf course there at Lake Martin, there were all the recreational pleasures of the big beautiful lake. I loved to boat with Dianne at the lake, and canoe up the streams, go out on the dock and watch the sunsets in this beautiful location.

After my stroke, however, this all changed. Dianne had sold my prized 21 foot Boston Whaler, when one of the doctors told her that I would probably never walk or talk again and one of my friends, Eddie, who really liked the Whaler, said he would buy it. Eddie Levin, one of my black belts, and his wife Sandy had gone with us to Costa Rica one year to go fishing and look at some investment property. We had a wonderful time together during that two-week jaunt. In addition, Eddie had gone out on Mobile Bay with me many times in the Whaler and really liked the way it handled.

I was lucky to get up to Lake Martin that first year. I could then only sit on the porch and look at the lake, watch the sailboats, the jet skis, and the fishermen leaving in the morning. Walking a few steps without the wheelchair or walker was a challenge, but I managed to finally get to the clubhouse, about a half-mile, after about three days of pushing myself.

This past year, the walk to the clubhouse was no problem. I didn't have to stop, rest, or go back, as I had in previous years. At least I could see the progress each year. My trek was slow but steady. My gait was poor, but at least I now had a gait and was able to maintain it throughout the walk.

Dianne and I walked it daily and even ventured up the hill about half a mile one day. As I reflected, I realize there were many obstacles to overcome. Each stroke is individual, and each person must overcome his own obstacles as he regains his health. Some people will regain normalcy very quickly; these are the lucky ones who have light strokes. The difficulty with people who have more than just a mild stroke is the emotional and mental damage they suffer, which many don't see.

My cousin Smitty, whom I mentioned earlier, is about my age and had a very severe stroke that left him partially paralyzed and unable to speak. The physical effects are bad enough, but trying to cope with the mental anguish of not being able to communicate with those you love is extremely difficult and I knew the mental anguish he was dealing with because I had been there.

I had always admired Smitty as we were growing up and now even more. He was showing that the strength he had was not only physical, but mental as well. He had the stroke about two years before me, but, because we lived a thousand miles apart, I had not known about it. When I went back home to visit my mother in Dover, Delaware, I went to look him up.

He was trying to live and regain as much normalcy in his and his family's life as possible. His wife, Carol Horton is a real trooper, like mine. She had assumed all the duties of the house and home. On the outside you could not see much problem—Smitty looked fine—but inside I'm sure Smitty was like me, battling, agonizing and thinking... *will it be better tomorrow?*

Returning from a stroke is not a little bump in the road but a mighty mountain to climb. I was resolved to continue to work like hell in order to accomplish just that...if a blind man can climb Mount Everest, I should be able to climb back from this stroke!

Chapter 14

Getting Back on the Horse

The man who has no imagination has no wings.
Muhammad Ali

Five years post-stroke, I have completed my first acupuncture lecture in Dallas, Texas. I have lectures to give in Atlanta, Washington, D.C., and Birmingham. Then if I feel good and all seems to go well, I will accept a lecture contract of one lecture each month. Dianne and I feel this wouldn't be too hard on me. A group of physicians had asked me to do an acupuncture certification series. They would be holding the lectures in Orlando, which is only a few hours away in driving time and would be easier for me to get to than flying. Flying, with the waiting, the searches, and all the security since 9/11 and the War in Iraq is a real hassle now at the airports. I told Dianne that I thought I'd just stay close to home for now and do a few local lectures. The laser research I have gotten involved with over the past year and my writing that is so important to me now has got me back to the point "I feel like I have gotten back on the horse that threw me," as my grandmother would say.

With seeing patients five days a week, teaching Shorinji Kempo three nights a week, lecturing on weekends, I never had much time for writing much of anything but short professional articles and a few chapters in some textbooks. Now that I have retired from teaching Shorinji Kempo after 30 years, I am still an active member of the Zen Buddhist order Seiho Shorinji in Shikoku, Japan. But as stated earlier, I have finally faced reality and turned the physical teaching of the martial art over to my long time friend and assistant, Rusty Loftin. He is doing a great job, and I feel positive that classes will continue to grow.

I turned my chiropractic practice over to, a nice young husband and wife, chiropractors from Louisiana by the name of Renee and Kyle who wanted to settle down in the quiet little town of Fairhope to raise their family. I am continuing my therapy Mondays, Wednesdays, and Fridays at the local Wellness Center. In addition, I teach a class of physically challenged seniors at the Wellness Center.

This is a great class, with the youngest participant at about 65 and the oldest about 98. They are a lively and energetic group, though we do just about the entire class seated in chairs, with a few minutes at the end standing at a dance bar for practicing balance and strength.

I love this class, and all the people try really hard to get a good workout. Believe it or not I can work you pretty good from a chair. The heart rate is gradually increased about 50%, and the respiratory rate is increased. We do some chair raises to increase the strength of the thighs so they won't have such a difficult time getting up from a sitting position. During this phase, I teach them the proper biomechanics of sitting, standing, and walking. This is sustained for about 20 to 25 minutes, followed by a 10 minute cool-down that brings them back to a normal state.

My time with the seniors is special to me, I think, because it reminds me of my relationship with my grandmother. She was a remarkable woman. She still found the time to raise a wonderful family during the Great

Depression and went on to be a great teacher and inspired me to become a doctor and healer. She died at the grand old age of 97 in Dover, Delaware, where my family finally settled down. Her daughter, Nora Mae Stump, was my mother, who unfortunately died before this book could be published. My uncle, William H. Smith 'Rink,' is her youngest son and a WWII hero of mine. He has promised to tell me more history of my grandmother so I can at some point put a book together about her life. I shall never forget the ability she had to tell stories of the "Gold Rush Days" and "Blue Ridge" folklore as I was growing up.

    I remember going home after graduating from Palmer College of Chiropractic, I was then about 29 years old, to tell my parents I wanted to leave and go to China and Japan to study acupuncture. My father was very much opposed to it, and my mother wasn't in favor of it either. My father had lost two brothers in World War II and blamed the Japanese and Germans. My mother didn't seem to care about that so much as my being so far away for so long. But my grandmother, whose opinion I valued greatly, secretly whispered for me to go and learn as much as possible about healing, for they (the Chinese) have understood for thousands of years the secrets of healing. She told me she knew an old Chinese man who worked on the railroad back in 1897, who had told her about acupuncture and performed some in her presence. But he went on to California where he had family and she never saw or heard of it again. "Yes, go ahead to the Orient and bring back the secrets to help our people here in America," she told me.

    This I did. Over the next 20 years I ventured to the far corners of the world to learn the secrets of health and longevity that the American Medical Association and many western philosophies did not teach or adhere to. I left later in 1976 and went to Japan to study acupuncture and the martial art of

Shorinji Kempo. The adventure in the Orient where I learned that the historical texts, which refer to Japan as "the land of the happy immortals," is a whole other story that I will have to tell at another time. Suffice it to say, however, that I did get the many secrets of life and health and bring them back to America as my grandmother asked me to do when I journeyed to the Orient!

When I came back to America from my study abroad, it just seemed more accurate to treat people and correct their problems the fastest and the most conservative way possible. This turned out to be what is now called "integrative medicine." I called it "natural health care" for lack of a better term back then. Our first office, which we opened in Delmar, Delaware, in 1976, was called Delmarva Natural Health Centre and was the first of its kind on the Eastern Shore of Maryland and Delaware.

At that time I could not refer patients to a medical doctor or hospital or send patients for blood tests or X-rays. Our office had chiropractic, acupuncture, martial arts, yoga, tai chi, the Zen Den Café, and the Natural Foods Loft, so you can see we have had an integrative practice philosophy for the past 30 years. What I did was integrate Eastern and Western medicine for the benefit of the patient, because both are good and have their specialties.

I have been the owner and clinic director of eight practices during this period, three at one time on the Delmarva Peninsula. The remainder came later with my move south during my stint with the Olympic team from 1986 to 1988. This experience is what the doctors wanted to draw on to establish the Integrative Medicine Centre in Fairhope, Alabama. They wanted chiropractic, acupuncture, homeopathy, naturopathy and nutrition to work with traditional Western medicine for the benefit of the patient.

Integrative medicine has been a long time coming politically and still has a way to go, but I think the patients and the doctors are ready if we could just move the political machine along a little faster. The new location is now open in Fairhope and the patients love it.

As for me, I'm not sure if I'll make much more progress physically. There seems to be a little more at times, but realistically there has not been much for the past year. The real progress has been in my emotional acceptance of the fact I will always be somewhat physically limited. I now know that I can deal with this and still live a good life. Yes, it is different, but that's not to say it is not good. I have a loving and supportive wife, family, and friends. This proves to me that it can be done if one just keeps working at it with a positive attitude.

An Aspen Valley Holiday

After getting the Integrative Medicine Centre open, Dianne and I felt we needed a break. Gayle, her friend since our graduate school days at the United States Sports Academy in Daphne, Alabama, was now living in the Aspen area—specifically, in Basalt, a small town a few miles northwest-- of Aspen. Gayle had visited me shortly after the stroke. Actually, I did not know she was there at all because of just coming out of the coma and my mind not working very acutely at the time. She had kept up with my progress through Dianne. She realized it had been four or five years since she and her husband Bob had seen us. She had asked Dianne if she thought I could travel enough for a trip and visit to Colorado. If so, they would like to have us for a holiday vacation. We discussed it, and I felt Dianne deserved a holiday break and vacation. After all, she had been under as much pressure as I had, actually more, for I really was not cognizant of much of anything for the first year or two after the stroke when Dianne had the most stress.

We landed at Denver International Airport where Gayle met us. We would go from Denver to Basalt by car. She said it was about a four-hour drive, so we could drive to Idaho Springs, eat lunch, and then go on to Basalt. That sounded like a plan we could handle, so off we went in Gayle's Jeep.

The ride was wonderful and the scenery was beautiful with the magnificent mountains, tall Douglas firs, blue spruce, and the famous aspens that looked so much like our birch trees. I'm not sure if Dianne and Gayle saw much of anything, as they were so busy talking and catching up.

We soon arrived in Idaho Springs, a small mountain town that Gayle particularly liked. We decided to eat at a quaint restaurant famous for their buffalo burgers and great buffalo chili. Dianne and I, of course, had to try the local cuisine and I must admit it was quite good. After a brief look around the town we were on our way west again. It was more of the same for them talking about cooking, baking and decorating. They even came up with the idea of putting a cookbook together of Southern recipes from Dianne's background and cooking experience and Gayle's Southwest experience, since she was from Texas. I listened to them awhile but I couldn't get enough of this magnificent landscape. I had been to Colorado several times but never was it so beautiful.

Soon we were turning into the Altamira Ranch. A ranch that Bob's father started many years ago. As we crossed the bridge across the Roaring Fork River, I could see a big change since being there a little over four years earlier. There was now a golf course, with small log cabins with stone walks and fireplaces, tucked into the trees and hills scattered around the course. They had sold their ranch to a company that wanted to create an upscale golf getaway near Aspen. They had retained about ten acres where their house, barn, workshop, etc., was located.

I saw the cedar–sided, three-story house when we opened the gate. The last time I had seen the place they just had the basic structure up, and we had stayed in Bob's mother's bed-and-breakfast. Bob's mother was now in her nineties and had been an elementary school teacher in Aspen for many years before retiring to Basalt and starting the B&B.

The house had turned out great. It was a circa-1890 barn structure that had been built in Vermont originally. Bob had it moved here and reconstructed the entire barn. He and Gayle had done a marvelous job turning it into a beautiful home, which had taken a total of seven years to complete. Bob, a former photographer for Time-Life magazine and a real craftsman himself, gave me many of the details of the house. Since my father had been a craftsman and builder, I was familiar with terms and details of resurrecting the house from its original structure.

We had a great time going four-wheeling in the Jeep up into the mountains around Mount Sopris, Redstone, Marble and Crystal River. Add to that a trip to Durango, a train trip to the old mining town of Silverton, and a cookout by a real western campfire was just what we had needed to get rid of some of our stress.

Sightseeing and attending Rotary meetings in the towns around Aspen, such as Basalt, Carbondale and Glenwood Springs, the home of Doc Holliday, was more interesting than Aspen itself. Though Aspen is the more popular ski destination for many in the winter and home to many stage and film stars, they all seem to come down to earth when they are here in the Aspen/ Basalt area, Bob reported.

We had fun just sightseeing up through McClure pass and down to the two small mining towns of Redstone and Marble located in the beautiful Crystal River Valley. The Crystal River, which originates at Schofield Pass, is fed by melting snow and crystal clear springs, hence its name. The river passes through some of the most spectacular scenery in the Rockies as it flows by the ghost towns of Schofield and Crystal City on its way to Marble and Redstone. We had lunch at the famous Red Stone Inn, and it was outstanding. We visited the Red Stone Castle and many of the Victorian cottages in Red Stone that are now shops. We also visited Fryingpan Lake and river, one of the best trout streams in the country, Ruedi Reservoir, the Continental Divide and a host of other places it would take a whole chapter to tell you about.

Somewhere along the way Gayle said something that I couldn't get out of my mind. She commented on how wonderfully I was progressing. She commented the last time she had seen me in Alabama, right after my stroke, she never thought I would be back for a visit or be able to do the things we had done, like climbing into the Jeep, four-wheeling on mountain trails, and cooking out. The physical impairment on my right side remained, yet I was getting around without a wheelchair or a cane. I was able to talk normally and, for all practical purposes, astonished her with my progress.

It was then that Dianne and I realized all the hard work and rehabilitation I had been doing for the past five years had paid off. We had been so close to the problem every day we could not see the progress but Gayle could. She had not seen me since the first month or so after the stroke and my change was dramatic to her. Gayle could not believe I actually was able to sit at my laptop and work on this manuscript at their beautiful ranch while she and Dianne went for long walks along the Roaring Fork River (originally called Thunder River by the Ute Indians) catching up on the years they had missed.

I really was not sure how I was going to make out on this trip to the Rockies, with uneven footing, rough terrain and high steep mountains. I can honestly say I was pleasantly surprised to find it was a wonderful trip with no real problems. Colorado, Gayle, and Bob were perfect hosts and will see us again...if they will have us!

Writin' n' the Rockies
"Altamira Ranch"
Gayle & Bob's house
Basalt, Colorado -2003

A Stroke of Midnight...

Chapter 15

Family, Friends and Others

A man travels the world over in search of what he needs and returns home to find it.
George Moore

You may think the relationship with your family, relatives, and friends won't change once you have had a stroke, but that will probably not be the case. I know from experience now that much has changed in our social circle.

For instance, just after the stroke, a lot of people paid their respects but most believed the doctors were right, I would never walk or talk again. The fact I had lived, can walk and talk was a miracle, they thought.

I have lived away from most of my family for the past 20 years, with them in Maryland and Delaware and me in Florida, Iowa, South Carolina, Maryland, Japan, China, Korea, Alabama, and other places. Because of this separation, it is hard to have an opinion on their reaction to the stroke. For the most part, though, I believe they accepted it and have treated me no differently.

I have, however, noticed a change in many of my friends. Now that I am cognizant of how people react to my physical impairments and the way I talk, many previous friends—or should I say acquaintances—no longer come around or are "available" for social interaction. I did not notice this at first because of my mental and emotional concentration on recovery. In other words, I was too absorbed in the process of trying to get better to stop and worry about how I was affecting my friends...I was fighting for survival!

Some of them came by to take me to a football or baseball game or some other event, and I had to have assistance getting in and out of the vehicle, both when I was in the wheelchair and after I was ambulatory. It was then I noticed for the first time I was never asked to go again. Even the close friends who came to the hospital to visit and stay with me no longer come around. I think it's the fact they don't want to be responsible if I fall or something happens because I'm impaired now. We Americans are such a litigious society today even friends protect themselves legally against other friends when they can. I think I fit into this category with many of my old friends now that I have had a stroke.

It's not that they don't like me any more. I realize I am not capable of doing the things I once could do. I want everyone to know I understand this and can live with this result. They don't have to worry. I'm not angry or hostile for having had a stroke. I realize that I must pick up my life at this point and carry on from here.

The one thing I am grateful for is that people are not condescending and overprotective of me. My wife is my primary caregiver at this point and always has been except when I was in the hospital. People around her treat her as they did before the stroke. In not changing their behavior, Dianne's friends aren't showing disrespect, nor are they indifferent to her plight. Rather, they indicate that they respect what she has accomplished with the problems I've had. Except for going to our son Chad's wedding, Dianne has never left my side. She treats me with respect and compassion; she knows I want to do many things I can no longer do, but she lets me make that decision.

The physical damage I have suffered from this stroke has been extensive, and my dysfunctions are obvious. The psychological damage has been minimal even with my years of rehabilitation. I have had no preconceptions or assumptions about my lost capacities and opportunities. I realize I had a stroke at the peak of my career, and I know it will now limit my opportunities for further career goals. But I am glad it did not lead to any lasting damage that will impede the recovery of the self-esteem and self-empowerment that is so important to a stroke survivor.

I was reminded by my friend Sue Moore, of how at one time I had to ask her to be sure to remind me of any important events that were coming up; birthdays, anniversary, holidays, because I couldn't remember due to the stroke but, now I can remember!

Unlike many stroke survivors, I think I have been able to make the best of the circumstances. I figure you must play the cards you are dealt in life, and this was my hand! I feel my marriage has actually solidified. Dianne and I have been able to reach new levels of intimacy and love. Our lovemaking has become an exciting new adventure. Dianne will not admit to being an angel, but in my opinion she is as close to one as I'll find here on earth.

I feel my attitude toward the stroke has been helpful in helping other people to understand the effects and ramifications of the situation, as when I tell my friends or students I still have trouble at times reading and speaking. They know I can read and love to read, but getting the words out is still difficult . When time constraints are important I will explain my reading difficulty since my stroke and have one of the students read the specific text aloud instead of doing it myself. I have even thought about this book being published. There are book readings and book signings - well that's going to be another challenge for me!

Many of my fellow stroke survivors are less fortunate. The stroke experience often puts close relations to the test and not all friends are willing or able to be patient enough to be supportive and sensitive in the range of activities that they can share at a given time. The very essence of friendship is often challenged at the point when a stroke survivor asks for help from a longtime friend. Some are up to the challenge, and this actually makes the friendship grow richer as a result of the support the friend provides. But there are others who will not be able to handle the change; they will feel uncomfortable around the person who has suffered a stroke and will break off the relationship. My professional friends have probably been the most difficult to understand. I learned many had heard I had died or I was near death. Well, even if the latter had been true, I am now back and ready to go on doing something beneficial for others. However, even though they sent their cards and letters with their condolences, they seemed to have already written me off as a viable member of the profession.

A few years ago when I was searching for ways to fill my semi-retired time, I was without what I needed most, the feeling of self-worth and self-esteem that had driven me so hard before the stroke. Out of a desire to regain this feeling, I wrote to many of my professional associations to see if I could volunteer my services. After all, I had four doctoral degrees and plenty of free time. I never heard from any of them, and I assumed they had all written me off as another stroke case that was of little professional value.

This was not the case, however. A colleague told me later that many within the professional circles knew the drive, motivation, and determination I had. They did not want to ask me to return to professional life before I was ready physically and mentally. They knew what a devastating ordeal the stroke had been because they had been in contact with my wife and family. They knew I needed the time to have proper rehabilitation and that I would return when I could.

Now, I have been able to lecture again, attend conferences and professional meetings, do research, consult with patients, and do more writing. My colleagues have welcomed me back again to the extent I can be involved; they know and I know there is a limit to my commitment.

Healing

Many people ask me about the process of healing. The fact that I have been a healer for the past 30 years is a blessing. It is a blessing that I have witnessed thousands getting better as a result of methods I chose to use to help the ill and incapacitated.

I traveled to the far corners of the globe to try to find the ultimate natural healing methods for our human ills. In many cases what I learned was the answer; for some it was not. I learned there is no one key that fits all the locks of healing. I was a miracle worker for some who would come in the office unable to walk and crying in pain and then walked out with little or no pain.

My problem when I think back on my career as a doctor was trying to constantly "prove" the energy medicine that I practiced. From a scientific viewpoint, one problem with energy medicine is the challenge of creating the concrete proof that the energy system really exists. Trying to prove that there is an energy system with the acupuncture meridian points for example, is much like trying to prove that gravity or energy in general exists. You can't see it, but intuitively you know that it's there and you can create tests that will verify its existence, but it never seemed to be enough proof for the scientist.

Early findings by Yale University researcher, Harold Saxon Burr in his work on the "Aura" (1972) pointed out electromagnetic fields. He called these energy fields "Life fields."

Another pioneer in the field of energy medicine, Richard Gerber (1988), author of *Vibrational Medicine* writes that physical disease may begin at the energy level and then migrate into or show up in the physical body at a later stage. What Gerber is suggesting is indeed an ancient acupuncture principle taught to every acupuncturist in his or her study of the human body.

Therefore, if disturbances can be detected at the energy level before physical problems develop, treatment methods in time will emerge that can alleviate the energy disturbance and thus prevent the physical stroke or cardiovascular disease from ever occurring.

This is why I feel that my career was so blessed and my practice always thrived. I learned early from the acupuncture masters in the Orient how to detect and evaluate this energy in the individual. It was another blessing that I was a Chiropractor and understood the art of palpation (feeling) when I started the study of acupuncture and Oriental Medicine. It didn't take long for me to realize in Chiropractic College how important developing the art and skill of manipulation really was in practice. It didn't seem to matter much about which technique was used for correction after you found the Subluxation (malposition/misalignment). The Subluxation can be corrected numerous ways. Of course you don't realize this in school, there you think that technique is the most important part of your practical skills.

There were thousands of cases that came to me as a last resort but I seemed to have the key that they needed. Examples of some of the cases include the patient whose doctors told her she was now facing surgery of the colon for her abdominal pains. But, she didn't. After 10 acupuncture treatments she was 90% better. Then there was the man who came to me after his third surgery to remove a plantar wart. After 12 treatments he was delighted…no more pain or Plantart's wart. And the woman, who could not sit or lie down without extreme pain after having her coccyx surgically removed because of low back pain, was helped in a little over a month of treatment. So was the woman who had intractable headaches daily for 20 years after childbirth. Ancient acupuncture helped her in eight weeks.

For all of these patients and thousands of others, I was their miracle doctor, yet for others it was my colleague down the street or even in the same office who might be the healer of choice. The main thing was they had the opportunity for help.

These and many like them kept coming to me for 30 years because I could help them. But, there were those who remained my patients, who refused to get well or regain their health. That's when I felt practice was a curse because I knew what was going to happen and there was nothing I could do about it until they decided to help themselves.

These patients included the smoker who told me he wanted to quit and knew he had to quit or face the potential of death in a short time but did not stop until he was in the hospital on a respirator. Or the person who complained every time I saw them about their back hurting and knew I did chiropractic but would never come to the office to see if they could be helped. Or the person at my wellness center who told me his wife had to have countless orthopaedic procedures and none have helped but they do not have insurance to cover the cost of my service. There were those that could not afford services that I wish I could have helped. While I was with the International Chiropractors Association we did travel to Africa, India and several other countries giving our services away but could not afford to do this but one or twice each year for a week or two at a time.

These and many more examples were the reason I felt being a doctor was at times a curse as well as a blessing. Of course, this is probably true with many professions, but it really rang true with me so many times over the years. But, I was now in a situation where I could understand both the healer's perspective and the patient's perspective as well. I believe this is why many people still seek my counsel. I have been so close to death and now understand what it takes to return from that awful state. That is why I hope this book will help those who have suffered a stroke to advance on through the trials and tribulations on the road back to sanity, safety and security.

I also hope the information provides the general population with an understanding of the potential for stroke and the consequences. Of all the people you meet 50% are potential victims. I don't want others to have to experience the same things I did. Remember the best treatment for a stroke is never to have one!

Chapter 16

My Caregiver's View

Whoever is spared personal pain must feel one called to help in diminishing the pain of others.
Albert Schweitzer

[In this chapter I yield to my wonderful wife Dianne, who will give her perspective on the care of the stroke survivor.]

Many people have asked, "How long does it take to recover from a stroke?" The experts say that neurological recovery tends to reach a zenith within the first few months then taper off. In general, the earlier the recovery begins, the better. John's case was a little different because his doctors spent four months looking for his reason for the stroke, which turned out to be the pheochromocytoma. They did the surgery, and then it was like his recovery had to begin all over again. Actually his progress never was as good after the surgery. Even though the tumor was found to be benign, he never seemed to regain the physical recovery he had achieved before the surgery.

Let me discuss some of the areas that I feel are the most important to understand in caring for an individual who has suffered a stroke. Remember that you are going to have less personal time, you may face some role reversal, and you will have a great deal more responsibility and pressure. Just be prepared!

Personal Cleanliness

When the person returns home from the hospital after having a stroke, you may find that maintaining hygiene is awkward and difficult at first. Having the proper bathroom facilities is essential and makes life much easier. The products and accessories that are to be used each day should be laid out for the person to see and to learn to use again. He may not even recognize a simple thing like a toothbrush at first. It took John a month to learn his new home toiletry routine. Like brushing his teeth with the left hand instead of the right.

You may have to get adaptable items, for each individual will have his own restrictions and capabilities. I know that soap, bottles, and many things that we do not think of are difficult for them to grasp. They will find it hard to replace the caps on toothpaste tubes or shampoo bottles. A tube or bottle with a pump or attached flip-top may work better.

Shaving was one of the most difficult tasks that John had to or wanted to master again. Because John had formerly shaved with a straight razor, he wanted to try to accomplish this, but I finally talked him out of that and into at least using a safety razor. So, if you are the caregiver of someone who is capable and cooperative, leave well enough alone. If he is unable to manage personal hygiene on his own, be prepared to help as much as possible, but let him do as much as he can on his own.

Another item that was difficult for John was nightwear. He had always slept in the buff and so was not used to having any clothes on at night. Getting him to wear a hospital gown and a robe was very difficult once he was conscious. Try to look for clothes that have Velcro closures and clothes that do not have to be pulled over the head. This will make changing much easier, for both the caregiver and the stroke victim.

Safety Concerns

This is probably foremost in everyone's mind when a person is incapacitated in any way. As the caregiver you must think about and always put safety first in your mind. This was another area where John needed constant care; because he had always been rough-and-ready, he didn't seem to realize that now there was a decreased sensation in his right arm and leg. Besides falling several times when he had promised to stay on the porch, he was found once up in a tree trying to cut a dead branch that was hanging down over the driveway. Also, all glass containers must be replaced with plastic. Hand slippage and grasping problems are inevitable. It's better to err on the side of caution when thinking about avoiding cuts and abrasions.

The paralysis and weakness of his right side was very difficult to get John to understand. He knew that he had had a stroke, but he did not understand the limitations this imposed on him physically. I still have trouble making him understand that he must be extra-careful when doing simple tasks such as turning around. Because one side of the body does not respond as quickly as the other, a fall can happen easily. That is why handrails are so important. It seems like just holding onto or touching something gives the stroke survivor the added security needed.

Cognitive Concerns

This was an area of great concern for me as well as others who had known John before the stroke. He was always outgoing and paid attention to everyone and everything around him. When he came home, he was withdrawn, had trouble concentrating and didn't want to make any decisions in regard to anything. This was totally unlike John, so I just gave him some time and room for growth and repair, and he came around to his old self within a few months. John was the academic type that liked to read and write but after the stroke all he wanted to do was sit and watch TV. Then one day he seemed to change and wanted to go get a laptop computer and now he spends every spare minute at his desk.

Personal Relationships

There are few who can say that this area is not affected when a stroke occurs to a spouse who may be the primary caregiver. In most cases John had always been extremely loving, affectionate and sexual before the stroke, but for several months afterward there was no hint or indication of any desire for intimate physical contact. One day I asked him if there was something wrong with me; was I no longer desirable to him? He laughed and said no, that was not the case at all, if any thing it was he that was not desirable any longer.

The real problem was that John did not think he should physically perform for fear he might have another stroke. His stroke had occurred just minutes after a very intimate and loving evening after dinner. I told him I didn't think that was the case and we would speak to the doctor about his concern. On our next visit we talked openly about having sexual relations and whether this was any problem for him now. The doctor reassured him that everything would be just fine, that the only reason for the stroke was the tumor on his adrenal gland and now that it was taken care of, there was nothing to be concerned about in that department. That evening John was a totally different person and has been ever since; he makes sure things are well taken care of in that area now. He is even more caring and loving than he was before. And he takes special pride in not forgetting special occasions like birthdays, anniversaries, holidays, and vacations or getting me gifts and flowers.

When we first got John home from the hospital, he was still wrestling with the problem of paralysis and weakness. This was very difficult for him because he had always been so strong physically and mentally. He had always been independent and never wanted help doing things if he could avoid it. It didn't take long for him to realize that he might need help with things that he had never had trouble with before. But again I gave him the time and space to realize that I was not making him do something against his wishes but assisting him in the task that he could not manage.

I remember when he first came home; he had the most difficulty tying his shoes. I would suggest loafers or a shoe that would slip on, but no, John wanted his old favorites. Well, I just let him go a few weeks spending 10 or 15 minutes on each shoe. Then one day I just set a new pair of slip-on athletic shoes beside the old tie shoes that he loved. He came out of the bedroom just raving about how wonderful the new shoes were and asking why I hadn't suggested something like this before! I just had to laugh because he knew that I had tried and tried, but he was just not ready to concede defeat from those lace-up shoes until then.

Self-esteem is a problem for many after a stroke, but this was never a problem for John. He was always open and would talk about issues and problems with everyone. He never had any problems with self-esteem, self-worth or self-confidence. I guess being a doctor helped in this regard, but I know others have a great deal of difficulty with this issue with their spouse or loved one.

There was a time when John had a great deal of difficulty trying to face the reality of not being able to regain his physical capacities. If there was ever a time when John faced depression, this was it. He was always so positive and upbeat, but when the neurologist told him that if he had not gotten back the use of his right arm and leg after three or four years, he more than likely would not, John went into a tailspin for several months. He just didn't want to face the reality that he could not overcome something physical. He had always been able to bounce back from so many terrible physical conditions in the past that he thought he could do it again this time.

After several months of feeling down and not as jovial as usual, he said to me that he just couldn't wait for his body to make the rest of the repairs; he wanted to return to living as normal a life as he could with what he had. Since that day he has not been what I would call depressed; he has faced the fact that he will now always have a physical limitation on the right side of his body.

He is now a fighter for the rights of the physically and mentally handicapped and has given several lectures on this subject. He has chaired the heart and stroke benefit race the local hospital conducts each year. He is now proud to be called a stroke survivor, for he sees just how fortunate he is in regaining most of his abilities. What he has been able to accomplish is simply amazing.

Legal and Financial Issues

This is always a big concern when a crisis such as a stroke happens to a family member, especially when it happens to the primary breadwinner of the family. When this happens, there are many arrangements to take care of: finances, wills, health insurance, and other types of insurance. Yet many banks, credit card companies, and other institutions do not want to talk to you unless your name is on the dotted line. Explain the circumstances and find out what you must do to get the business matters settled and to assure your own security.

John always had me take care of the finances of the office and home. My primary duty was that of being the administrator of the corporation and in this regard I knew most all of the financial issues that had to be taken care of. Once "power of attorney" was taken care of, I was very familiar with the other matters.

This is not the case with many of my friends. They say that their home is run just the opposite, which everything is in his name and he takes care of all the financial matters. If this is the case you need to sit down and ask your husband many of these questions and have them written down where if something did happen you would be able to manage the household.

Self-Care Issues

John always had a saying he learned somewhere in the Orient that went something like "Live half for yourself and half for others." But the second half is not possible without the first. You must keep yourself as healthy and strong as possible so the task for others can be met. It is important to face the aftermath of the situation as early as possible. Don't let guilt rule; concentrate on the future and not the past.

Understand that the caregiver (you) needs a break occasionally, some personal time and time alone. Don't hesitate to ask for help. Many friends and family members want to help but must be told what is needed before they can act. Talk with your family and close friends about your feelings and fears. Many friends like Sue and Randa in the office really helped through this period more than they will ever know.

Don't be afraid to show emotion, because some of the issues that have to be faced are almost overwhelming at times and need to be vented. If not, the caregiver may reach a burnout stage and have to be taken care of as well. At this stage, depression often becomes an issue for the caregiver, who then must seek medical help.

Make sure you have given yourself time to grieve for your loved one. This may be a spouse, parent, or any other family member. You must come to terms with the situation and know that this is a temporary loss, or in some cases a permanent loss, that must be faced before a new future can be built for you and the stroke survivor.

Medical Issues

Always stay in close contact with the medical department at the hospital where the stroke survivor was last attended or with your private medical staff. Ask the doctor what to expect and have him teach you the skills you may need to give medical care at home. However, be aware of any medical complications that may arise and what should be done at that time. You must know when to call the doctor or take

the individual to the emergency room at the local hospital. These include problems such as:
- Weakness or numbness in previously normal parts of the body
- Shaking of one or more limbs
- Swelling or pain in a leg, arm or hand
- Severe sudden headache
- Unexplained pain
- Loss of consciousness
- Blood in the urine, especially if blood thinners have been prescribed
- Bleeding from the gums
- Side effects of medications
- Unusual behavior

Ask questions of the medical staff whenever you do not understand something. In particular, you should know:
- The symptoms of a stroke and what to do if it happens
- What to do in a medical emergency
- What can be done to help with medical treatment

Let the staff know your feelings about a situation, follow a healthy plan for yourself, and ask the doctor when you need something.

Recreation and Social Occasions

In scanning the literature, I know social interaction is one of the greatest difficulties that the stroke survivor faces in the days following the return home. It is of utmost importance to the stroke victim and caregiver alike. Crafts, hobbies, and recreational activities must be resumed when at all possible. Often these must be adapted to accommodate the loss of use of a limb or being in a wheelchair. It is understandable that a survivor will be restricted by new limitations, but it is very important for each to try and get out of the house to talk and meet others involved in daily activity. It will do you good to realize that both of you have problems you must work out, and it helps to talk to others in this process.

John was very physical being a former high school and college athlete and a black belt instructor. Even in his 50's he loved physical activities and sports. The stroke kept him from many of his favorite activities like martial arts, scuba diving, and running triathlons but introduced him to other interests that he soon accepted. Art, writing, reading and travel for pleasure were now going to take the forefront of his interest and he knew and accepted this change. John had trouble in school because he seemed to like everything. His interest is so wide he never had time to pursue any one thing like he wanted to. This is how he ended up with so many educational degrees.

Chapter 17

Preventive Medicine

The human capacity to fight back will always astonish doctors and philosophers. It seems, indeed, that there are no circumstances so bad and no obstacles so big that man cannot conquer them.
Jean Tetreau

This is a chapter you will not find in most stroke survivors' stories. I include it in honor of my mother-in-law, Myrtle Bearden, and dedicate it to her and my fellow Rotarians and the millions of others just like them who have suffered or may suffer Trans Ischemic Attack (TIA) episodes, or what is called pre-stroke incident. I am a Rotarian and love the Rotary philosophy, what they do, what it stands for, and where it is going. I have always traveled a great deal and it alarmed me every time I would go to the many different clubs as visiting member. Let me explain, most Rotary meetings are held at breakfast (7 AM) or lunch (Noon) at restaurants and dinner for special occasions. I have attended meetings in many states and foreign countries over the last two decades and at the end of this chapter you will understand what I mean about being alarmed at the consequences of the Rotary meetings.

The Rotarians have the prudence to take on national disasters like the *Tsunami, Mudslides,* and *Katrina,* not one at a time but all three at once in different parts of the world. The Rotary is a powerful force of human trust, kindness, and benevolence throughout the world. What I am about to explain and propose is within the capabilities of this great organization.

Earlier I stated, Coronary Vascular Disease (CVD) or coronary artery disease is the most common type of heart disease, and is the leading cause of death in the United States for both men and women. The coronary arteries supply blood to the heart muscle, and CVD occurs when the arteries become clogged with fatty deposits called plaque. The term Coronary Artery Disease is also used in this book interchangeably with cardiovascular disease (CVD). Every 45 seconds, a person in the United States has a stroke as a result of CVD. It is one of the most catastrophic medical events to befall an individual, and it is also one of the most preventable! As plaque builds up, the arteries harden and become narrowed (atherosclerosis), subsequently reducing blood flow to the heart. In turn, this decreases the oxygen supply to the heart and can cause chest pain (angina). If a blood clot forms, it can suddenly cut off blood flow in the artery and cause a heart attack. If the clot breaks off and flows to the brain it can cause a stroke. Over time, CVD can weaken the heart muscle and lead to ineffective pumping of blood to the body (heart failure) and changes in the normal rhythm of the heartbeats (arrhythmias).

The current research seems to indicate that cholesterol is not the culprit in strokes as much as some other risk factors. Of course the best treatment for stroke is never to have one. Some experts feel the way you prevent that is to eliminate the possibility of diabetes and hypertension and again this is related back to lifestyle, diet, and exercise.

William Lee Cowden, MD, has published the fact that if a patient can be treated within the first 12 hours after a stroke with a combination of essential fatty acids, a high antioxidant intake, and either hyperbaric oxygen therapy or ozone therapy, a dramatic regression of symptoms of the stroke will occur. But, how realistic is this? I know when I had my stroke, even though I had an idea in my mind what was happening, I couldn't talk. Dianne and the EMS crew were just trying to get me to the hospital to save my life. Plus, it took them days not just hours to accomplish controlling bleeding in the brain, resulting in a coma for weeks after the stroke. Do you really think that fatty acids, antioxidants or even hyperbaric chambers are the first thoughts when it comes to taking care of a stroke victim? I think Dr. Cowden is reporting something that should have been done by the stroke victim years prior to the stroke incident, when risk factors started to appear in their lifestyle. You can't expect a patient or their family to try to rationalize taking the person suspected of having a stroke anyplace other than to an emergency room at the nearest hospital.

This is the reason I have included this chapter that is so important. Prevention is ***not*** an emergency reaction. It is a long-term lifestyle change to prevent an emergency like a heart attack or a stroke from occurring.

Some of the latest available statistics from the World Health Organization (WHO) regarding the main causes of death in Europe, the United States, and other industrialized countries in this new millennium are staggering.

Every year more than 12 million people worldwide die from atherosclerosis, heart disease, and stroke. These are by far the most common causes of death in our time. The answer to this epidemic of stroke and heart-related disease conditions is prevention. Based on the knowledge we have today, heart disease and stroke can be reduced to a fraction of the current figures if people would begin to understand that heart disease starts with the food that we eat.

The most common diseases and causes of death in developing countries are infectious diseases like measles and malaria, and HIV/AIDS. The three leading causes that are found in the industrialized nations: CVD, cancer and stroke are not as common in developing countries. These diseases can only continue the way they do because the knowledge of prevention has not been efficiently used. This chapter will help provide some of the solution for the control of coronary disease. Although somewhat technical, I want to give you my opinion as well as that of several other experts in circulatory care and the relationship to stroke prevention.

Salt and Stroke

As far back as 1960, Lewis Dahl of Brookhaven National Laboratory, discovered that a high salt intake caused elevated blood pressure in some subjects but not in others. After some further research they found that some people are prone to or inherit high blood pressure problems and some do not even if they consume twice the normal amount of salt. Most of this research was done on rat populations at that time.

Some indirect evidence was gathered coming mainly from studies of different populations eating varying amounts of salt in their diets.

Some isolated tribes, such as the Kung Bushmen of the Kalahari Desert and the Yanomamo Indians of Brazil, consume diets extremely low in salt, generally less than 500 milligrams per day. Studies have found that these people experience no hypertension and that their blood pressures do not rise with age, as do those of people in industrialized societies. In contrast, farmers in northern Japan, who preserve food with salt, consume as much as 30 grams of salt each day (about six teaspoons). Approximately half of them had high blood pressure, and the most common cause of death was CVD and stroke.

Similar studies have been carried out in more than 20 cultures, ranging from Greenland Eskimos to natives of the Solomon Islands in the South Pacific. Taken together, the studies show that hypertension is rare in populations that use very little salt. Conversely, in societies where a lot of salt is consumed, a significant number of the people develop the disease.

These studies *suggest,* that salt intake is related to essential hypertension in humans. It is suggested by most experts that a moderate intake of salt has little clinical effect upon essential hypertension but most people should watch their salt and blood pressure all through their achieved lifespan.

Salt intake of African Americans may contribute to their stroke and death rate, and why they are 3-4 times more likely to suffer a stroke than white Americans or Latin Americans. African Americans as a group are less likely to receive or ask for information on how to decrease, prevent, or manage stroke, which also may increase the rates. Also, minorities as a whole lack health insurance and are less likely to receive preventive care. The rate of high blood pressure in African Americans is among the highest in the world: nearly one-third of black New Yorkers report high blood pressure, compared to nearly 20% of white New Yorkers.

Cholesterol

The incidence of high cholesterol with heart disease is common knowledge. Why is it a fact that many may run six miles a day, eat oat-bran for breakfast, lunch, and dinner and take blood pressure lowering medication, yet still wind up one of the 50% struggling with heart disease? Let me shed a little light on this.

Basically, the origin of low blood flow and coronary disease can be considered from two cellular aspects: (*a*) the lack of biological fuel needed by the cell's power plants, the *mitochondria,* and/or (*b*) a failure in the function of the nucleus, the metabolic control center of the cell.

In the lack of biological fuel in the power plants of the cell (mitochondria), coronary vascular disease (CVD), for instance, is mainly caused by an insufficient supply to the cell of biological fuel in the form of vitamins, minerals, and other cell factors. These nutrients are needed for the conversion of food into cellular energy, which is used by the cell in many metabolic functions. Another example is heart failure, which is caused by a lack of bio-fuel in the cells of the heart muscle. With low energy production, the pumping function of the heart muscle becomes impaired, causing shortness of breath and accumulation of fluids in the body. Generally, supplying of vitamins, minerals, enzymes and other bio-fuel will correct the impaired pumping function of the heart muscle and can help prevent CVD.

During the growth of atherosclerotic plaques (deposits), even in advanced stages of atherosclerosis, the process of prevention plays an important role.

It is generally known that, as in the sailors' disease scurvy, the initial step in the development of atherosclerosis is a lack of vitamins in the arterial wall. As a result of this vitamin deficiency the arteries of the heart weaken, which triggers a repair process to stabilize the walls of these blood vessels. Initially, the body mobilizes fatty particles (lipoproteins) and other repair molecules from the blood to deposit them in the weakest areas of the arterial wall.

When the repair measures become inadequate, the weakening arterial wall is further stabilized through an uncontrolled growth of the cells that build the vascular wall. These cells, called smooth-muscle cells, migrate from the outermost cell layer of the artery to the area that contains atherosclerotic fatty deposits.

Naturally, the effective approach in the prevention and treatment of "arteriosclerosis" (narrowing of the smaller vessels) is to preserve the integrity of the artery walls, which can be achieved through optimal vitamin, mineral, enzyme, and other cellular bio-fuel. Every therapeutic possibility that will halt this mechanism or even slow it down will therefore be of the utmost importance in preventing this coronary epidemic. This is why the first step is eating well and the second step is proper whole food supplementation of the diet until a better diet can be achieved.

Fatty Acids

Several recent studies have shown that the omega-3 fatty acid *eicosapantaenoic* (EPA) is a helpful factor in reducing platelet aggregation (clot forming) and thrombosis constituents. When given in a dietary supplement form as a mixture of oils from cold-water fish, there has been an observed beneficial effect of EPA in reducing platelet aggregation. EPA inhibits the formation of the prostaglandin *thromboxane A-2,* a potent vasoconstrictor that increases platelet aggregation. It also inhibits production of prostaglandins generally in platelets and arteries, further reducing overall platelet activity.

Omega-3 fatty acids also aid in the production of prostaglandin series PGE-3, known to lower LDL cholesterol and reduce the blood's tendency to clot. As the omega-3 fatty acid and EPA content of mainly cold-water fish is generally high, it is not surprising that many studies have shown that regular consumption of fish, particularly mackerel, salmon, and sardines, significantly lowers the development of atherosclerosis, CVD, and stroke. It is unfortunate but true, as the red meat consumption of the past century has increased and the fish consumption has decreased, and not surprisingly the incidence of CVD has markedly increased.

Genetics and CVD

Another interesting link is 'The Human Genome Sequencing Project.' It has been analyzing the nearly six billion pieces of DNA that make up our human inheritance. Perhaps the greatest discovery of this ongoing research to date has been the misunderstanding that many so-called "age-related" diseases, such as heart disease, Type 2 diabetes, and even certain forms of cancer, are inevitable. Rather than the previously held view that our genetic template is a map that determines our health future with no alteration possible, scientists are reaching a new understanding that altering our future health can be achieved by matching our genetic makeup to choices in diet, nutrient intake, exercise, and lifestyle that positively influence gene expression.

The fatalistic view previously held proposed that, regardless of the "right" choices people made with regard to cardiovascular health, such as following recommendations to lower blood cholesterol, reduce blood pressure, stop smoking, or lower dietary fat intake, many would still die "inevitably" of CVD because their genes said so. It is becoming increasingly clear that the "genomic" era of medicine is identifying important risk factors and needs associated with specific gene expressions. This indicates there is significant variation in how individuals respond to diet and lifestyle choices. We can see the merit in this by reading some of the latest research applications of diet by Dr. Peter J. D'Adamo, author of *Eat Right For Your Type,* and his work in foods and blood types. Thus, there is a synergy between those nutrients and our biochemical makeup that indicate we should continue to try to make the correct choices in the foods that we consume.

Trace Mineral Analysis (TMA)

A Trace Mineral Analysis is still a controversial technique of analysis. But, as I tell my patients, it is one good way of seeing where the body happens to be when it comes to the all-important minerals in the body tissues. The minerals can be normal in the blood but still deficient in the body tissues. We use a blood tissue to measure the short-term analysis and the trace mineral analysis or hair analysis, as the test is commonly called, to measure the long-term level of the tissue health. This is a very important step in the biochemical and metabolic understanding of the body tissues.

The electrolytes, calcium, magnesium, sodium, potassium and phosphorus are usually the first minerals that need to be balanced and understood. That's why a blood test to check the level of the electrolytes is one of the fist things ordered in the hospital. There are many important minerals that must be evaluated after the electrolytes are brought into normal range.

Another important part of preventive medicine is that of nutritional evaluation of toxic heavy metals such as, lead, mercury, cadmium, arsenic and aluminum. These should be eliminated and stay at a minimum in the body tissues. Other nutrient minerals can pose health problems like copper and manganese as well. Here are two prime reasons to use the

TMA system when considering a preventive program. It is important that a person understand that the foundation of the biochemistry in the human body begins with the minerals. That is why the electrolytes are generally checked right away. A TMA would simply follow up a blood sample with a profile to analyze the remaining body minerals, including the heavy toxic minerals.

These findings are helping usher in a new era of medical therapeutics, one of truly individualized care and treatment aimed at prevention through diet, exercise and lifestyle alterations matched to the unique individual.

We as a nation are beginning to see the practice of matching nutrient intake and lifestyle to the prevention and treatment of CVD and stroke. The complex nature of CVD and its prevention and treatment are certainly not limited to this chapter. There are numerous studies and ongoing research beyond the scope of this chapter that connect a number of functional processes ultimately related to CVD and stroke. Insulin resistance, the first step of diabetes is a part of the chemistry of the stress response and CVD, and the utilization of specific programs, such as the 'Ornish Diet,' a diet developed by Dean Ornish, MD and used for heart health without drugs or surgery. This diet is just one of several that has been studied for over a decade for the reversal of CVD with good results.

The updated guidelines for primary prevention of stroke continue to be studied. The rate and incidence issued have continued to climb. A bulletin May 2006 states that death from stroke has declined slightly over the last few years, but the incidence of stroke which afflicts about 700,000 people a year in the United States has declined only slightly less than 1%, according to the latest American Heart Association report. Nutrition factors are playing a greater role in the prevention of heart disease and stroke. A good nutritional program that includes vegetables, fruits, legumes, fish and whole grains is very important part of the prevention program.

Diabetes

There is an epidemic of type 2 diabetes cases across the nation and many experts feel that this is going to increase the incidence of strokes among middle aged adults and newly diagnosed diabetics. Collective research suggests that the latest warning of an impending health crisis that may be the result of the lifestyles of the people of America and western nations. This report was recently presented at a conference held in Florida by the American Stroke Association.

Type 2 diabetes is largely preventable through diet and exercise and afflicts an estimated 18 million Americans. Another 40 million have a condition known as pre-diabetes, which puts them at high risk for developing diabetes. About one-third of those with type 2 diabetes don't know they have it.

The surge of type 2 diabetes has closely followed the increasing number of overweight and obese individuals in America. In a Canadian study, researchers found that strokes were occurring in diabetics within five years of their diagnosis and new-onset diabetics have double the rate of stroke within the first five years of their diagnosis.

There are a number of theories as to why diabetes increases the risk of stroke. Yet research statistics over the last 10 years suggest a growing tendency and cumulative effect from the diabetes.

This is why my practice has taken a new turn and I am convinced doctors must understand and emphasize that diet is one of the most important basic facts that people have to learn about their health and to be much more selective about their food and drink choices.

Simply and tragically, there are no statistics in health care today more staggering than those for CVD. Cardiovascular disease is by far the number one cause of death, not only in America, but globally as well. Yes, a new day is dawning, a day of truly preventive health care, a time of truly energizing our very cells, maximizing the life force of our bodies. Foods contain nutrients essential for normal metabolic function, and when problems arise, they usually result from imbalances in nutrient intake and from harmful interaction with other lifestyle factors, smoking, excess drinking, drugs or improper sleep patterns. But, are people willing to take responsibility for their own health and make the necessary changes? The National Committee for Quality Assurance has emphasized prevention of cardiovascular diseases by advising people of the risk that we have already mentioned. Yet clearly the enormous number of deaths associated with CVD warrants more investigation and emergency action.

Answers to reducing the morbidity and mortality associated with stroke, cardiovascular disease, and death cannot lie only in developing costly and complex technological treatments. The procedures to prevent and alleviate the symptoms of the disease state must be emphasized as well. The health care profession must focus its attention on prevention of CVD and stroke, assisting individuals in taking greater responsibility for their health through diet, exercise, and related lifestyle changes.

Stress

Stress is an essential topic to discuss. Factors besides diet and exercise influence our health. There is increasing research to substantiate the theory that emotional stress can influence your risk of getting CVD. There are direct connections between the brain and vascular system. During stressful times, arteries constrict and blood may clot faster. This increases the risk of blood flow problems. Stress then can actually increase the rate at which blockages may clog up your arteries, independent of your diet.

How you handle stress can affect your cardiovascular health. If, for example, you reach for a cigarette to calm your nerves, this results in cumulative risk exposure since tobacco use is also a risk factor for CVD. The solution? Kicking the tobacco habit and finding another way to relax – exercise, indulge in your favorite hobby, get a massage, do some Yoga postures, or practice Zen meditation, or any type of meditation that suites your philosophy. Rather than smoke 7 minutes off of your life (the average time each cigarette takes off an individuals life) find a healthy stress reliever!

In a 2005 study published in the *Journal of Social Behavior and Personality,* researchers found that transcendental meditation (TM) can reduce blood pressure. Practicing TM or other forms of meditation for 20 –30 minutes twice a day has been proven to be beneficial to reduce stress. So, I am a firm believer in the benefits of meditation. Meditation is one of the pillars of the type of martial art (Shorinji Kempo) that I taught for years and another reason it has been so beneficial in the orient for so long. I no longer practice the physical aspect of the martial art but I continue the meditation aspect regularly.

Now, it is important here to review the ten steps to prevent a stroke.

Ten Steps To Prevent Stroke

1. Avoid smoking and over consumption of alcohol.
2. Don't use amphetamines, cocaine, or other illicit drugs as these may be harmful to your heart.
3. After age 50, have your carotid arteries checked every five years for atherosclerosis.
4. Monitor your blood pressure (optimal = *120/80).
5. Exercise daily, aerobic, flexibility and strength training.
6. Eat a variety of fresh, unprocessed fruits and vegetables daily.
7. Avoid trans fats, cholesterol, and sugar and keep your weight within 5-10 pounds of ideal to help prevent diabetes, which is detrimental to the heart.
8. Take whole food supplements of calcium, magnesium, vitamins E & C, organic minerals, and bioflavonoids and others if there are risk factors involved.
9. If female over 35, avoid birth control pills.
10. Get a yearly medical check up if over 40.

* This is only an average and varies for each person

Recognizing a Stroke

Even bystanders are easily able to recognize the symptoms of a stroke. Just follow these suggestions and you will educate others. The stroke victim may suffer damage when people nearby fail to spot the symptoms of a stroke.

A STROKE OF MIDNIGHT...

Now doctors say a bystander can recognize a stroke by asking three simple questions:

1. ASK THE INDIVIDUAL TO SMILE.
2. ASK THE INDIVIDUAL TO RAISE BOTH ARMS.
3. ASK THE PERSON TO SPEAK A SIMPLE SENTENCE (COHERENTLY).

If he or she has trouble with any of these tasks call 911 immediately, and describe the symptoms to the dispatcher.

Time for a New Health Care Era

It seems reasonable to ask, if the conventional medical protocol of prescription medication for CVD is failing to stop the ravages of the disease after decades of use, is there a better way? Can exercise, dietary and/or supplement therapies and lifestyle changes lower the risk and prevent CVD and stroke? The answer is a simple yes. Research in recent years has clearly shown that CVD and stroke are complex, with multiple disease categories defined within specific guidelines.

Much research and data suggest the benefits of prevention. However, it will never work unless people begin changing their lifestyles. The quickest and simplest way to begin is to eliminate processed foods from the diet as much as possible. This means everything from a can, box, or package (frozen or otherwise). I know that this is not easy for some of those who cannot get out to get fresh food each week. But you must reduce the oxidative stress on the body and the exposure to environmental pollution whenever and wherever possible. Cardiovascular disease and stroke are not simple, single diseases with a simple single solution. We can see that the present path of medicine is not controlling this epidemic and alternative paths need to be selected. We need to get back to nature as much as possible with our selection of foods, more exercise, and a better lifestyle!

Nutritional pioneers such as Dr. Royal Lee, Dr. Melvin Page, Dr. Weston Price, Dr. Frances Pottenger and many others worked diligently for many years to communicate the effects of poor nutrition and lifestyle on CVD and stroke. But unfortunately problems still exist in making Americans change their lifestyles.

There is a great deal of information available to the reader if you go to the back of this book and look for the references that apply to your interest. I have tried to reference as much of the material that I used and remember being helpful for others, as well as for me.

There are many scientific reports identifying the causes of heart disease. Some of our prominent mainstream doctors are now pointing to infections like Chlamydia pneumoniae (C. pneumoniae) as a factor in heart disease, and it is widely recognized that infections can trigger the formation of vulnerable plaque, leading to heart disease.

The bypass route that many heart specialists recommend is another reason for question. There are few if any studies on record to prove that bypass surgery works any better than other medical therapies. In fact, a 1984 study showed that after 11 years there was no difference between bypass and non-bypass patients.

Then how about the angioplasty method? It's slightly less invasive ...maybe a little less expensive ...but is it safer? No. There's a very real danger of the affected artery rupturing during the course of the procedure. Then the patient requires emergency bypass surgery anyway.

Western medicine is very good at identifying the problem. However, the issue is preventing CVD, not simply reacting to it. It is a matter of shifting the priority in medicine from treatment to prevention.

There's another heart care revolution I want to share. This system is really quite ancient in practice. Nutrition scientists have discovered a remarkable nutrient for heart tissues called Treminalia arjuna. Treminalia arjuna is from India and has been used for over 300 years. This is one of the health secrets that I told my grandmother I would bring back to our people here in America. Little did I know that the problem was getting people to understand how natural medicine actually works in the human body and to use it. Our citizens have been sold a pharmacological bill of goods. They think nothing works or is any good unless it comes from the corner pharmacy and works in a matter of hours.

There are a number of formulas that may be beneficial to the cardiovascular patient. Free radical damage to the arteries does not seem to be of interest to most physicians. This could be because there is no pharmaceutical answer to the free radical problem to date except better nutrition. Biochemistry shows that free radicals cause many problems in the body, especially premature aging of the cardiovascular system.

Many know and understand the importance of antioxidants such as Vitamin C and E, coenzyme Q-10, glutathione and Alpha-lipoic acid (ALA). There's one other thing I want to mention before we move on and that is to explain the function of homocysteine.

Homocysteine, an amino acid, has been identified by researchers as being one of the biggest precursors of heart problems. This is where the vitamin B family comes into play. Heart support is fortified with vitamins B-6, B-12, and folic acid and this trio actually help reduce homocysteine levels. In animal and human studies, L-arginine (another amino acid) has been shown to improve overall heart health. L-arginine may also help to lower body fat, increase muscle mass, help regulate insulin, support liver function, stimulate the thymus, and boost overall immunity.

People who supplement their daily diet with a good regimen of whole food supplements of antioxidants, B-vitamins, folic acid, L-arginine, and organic minerals tend to experience overall enhanced levels of energy. ***Warning: always check with your physician before taking nutritional supplements.***

There is evidence that Hawthorne berries and leaves have active ingredients known as procyanidins (a specialized group of flavonoid compounds) that have been shown to enhance cellular levels of adenosine monophosphate (AMP), a precursor of the ATP the energy-generating product in our cells. In Japan, Germany and other countries, supplementation with a standardized grade of Hawthorne has been shown in various well-designed studies to reverse congestive heart failure, lower blood pressure and improve cases of angina. In short, Hawthorn enables the cells of the body to make more ATP energy available. The Hawthorne is just another example of natural foods that are available for heart health.

What I have mentioned is just the tip of the iceberg when it comes to helping to reduce cardiovascular risk. There is so much that can be done. Since cardiovascular problems are said to be one of the most preventable self-induced diseases in modern history.

Individuals are vulnerable to their environments. The environment that we live in is another factor we must include here. The city and urban environment is no longer safe and healthy to walk or run for exercise, the toxic fumes from our automobiles are a cause for concern. The more affluent we become as a nation the more sedentary our people and children become. This has caused an obesity epidemic in America and many industrialized nations around the world. All of this increases the risk of CVD even more.

In my opinion, optimal cardiovascular health lies not in treatment after the fact of the many biochemical events that occur with poor nutrition and lifestyle, but in the early optimization and customization of the diet and lifestyle for all people through health education, beginning in elementary school. This message must now get to the young people.

This is the reason I am so concerned about my fellow Rotarians that are usually so aware and cognizant they have global and health concerns for others. What I would like to see is Rotary International take-on the prevention of cardiovascular disease, with the same energy and enthusiasm that they did polio in the past. If this were done, perhaps it could serve as an example for other organizations educating the public. Rotary meetings are unconsciously centered on food; breakfast, lunch or dinner meetings are always held. Because the meetings are usually at restaurants where, let's face it, generally the food is institutional at best. Yet, I have not heard one complaint about the food quality at any of the meetings I have attended around the country. Is this because Rotarians are not complainers? No, I don't think so. I think it is because the vast majority are not aware of the CVD epidemic and the connection of the diet of modern man. This is not a medical problem; primarily it is a public education problem. The general public has to become aware that 90 percent of CVD and stroke can be prevented if the correct diet, exercise and lifestyle changes are followed!!

Your age, sex, and genetic makeup influence your susceptibility to heart disease and stroke, and these factors are out of your control. However, many major factors that lead to CVD and stroke *are* within your control. As Paul Dudley White, the father of modern cardiology said many years ago, "Heart disease before 80 is your own fault." It is a medically accepted fact that daily living habits may determine if you're at risk of suffering CVD or stroke.

If you have a poor diet and are overweight, smoke, do not exercise, drink too much, and overreact to regular daily tensions and stresses in your life, you're a prime candidate for CVD. But you can change each of these undesirable habits if you're motivated to do so. You can beat the odds that CVD or stroke will strike you down!

Chapter 18

Tying It All Together

The worst thing in life may contain seeds of the best. When you can see crisis as an opportunity, your life becomes not easier, but more satisfying.
Joe Kogel

Here it is five years after my stroke and I'm just completing this manuscript. It could have been done sooner but I wanted to achieve as much recovery as possible according to the specialists working on my case. I have just completed consultation with two of the doctors, and they say little progress will be made from this point. I know there will be more, but it will be negligible according to their standards and measurements.

I have resigned myself to the physical limitations imposed upon my body from the remnants of this stroke. I am just glad I was able to regain my cognitive skills and was not damaged to the extent I have seen some of my stroke survivor friends. My recovery has been "remarkable" many have said when they hear the complete story. I would of course choose more recovery if it were my discretion but it was in God's hands I suppose. My recovery was from a near fatal stage, where I was unconscious for weeks, to about 90% recovery at the present time. At one time I never needed a microphone in a lecture hall; my voice was full and carried well. After this stroke my voice was not above a whisper for nearly a year but now my phonation is back to the reverberation and tone I once had. Shortly after acupuncture was introduced the pain I once had in my shoulder and hip was completely resolved. I continue acupuncture now each month to balance the energy of the body. Chiropractic maintenance is used in the same way except I need to be adjusted a little more by my Chiropractor, Dr. Gloria Dodds. My thinking has been pretty clear from the second year, even though Dianne may disagree due to my wanting to go back to the clinic and the work that would involve. I do not have to search for words as I once did and my short-term memory has just about all returned. I still can't recall some Japanese and Chinese and other languages that I knew. Maybe this is because I have just been so long at not using them. My vision was restored after about two months after the stroke and I've never had any problem since. The sense of taste and smell was never impaired like it is in some stroke victims although at times they thought it was by the way I didn't want some foods. Sue and Randa reminded me that before my stroke I had been a vegetarian (I did eat fresh seafood) and after the stroke I went back to eating meat again. Probably the most significant normalization to me was the restoration of my ability to whistle. When I could not even pucker and make a sound come from my mouth I knew I had trouble. About two years ago I was driving down the road going to Home Depot and an old favorite tune came on the radio and I just automatically started whistling …man was I happy. I am back to lecturing and teaching on a somewhat limited basis because Dianne does not want me to do too much and get back into the same routine that contributed to the stroke in the first place… a pheochromocytoma from working too hard. I never let up and kept relentless stress on myself, which caused the adrenal tumor. My right arm is still my most impaired limb. I can now lift my arm and move it in each direction but I have very limited use of my arm from the elbow down and any of my fingers. The physical therapist did tell me that the hand would be the last thing to be restored. I do have approximately 75 percent of my sensation back into my arm and hand. My leg is somewhat restored; however I still have a half-inch shorter leg on the right, which contributes to the limp that I have been left with after the stroke. I still walk with the "stroke gait" that everyone is familiar with. Plus not being able to move my right foot or toes does make balance a problem at times. Other than these impairments I am back to normal. I can do all the activities of daily life now and I even stay home unattended at times for weeks while Dianne visits the kids or our new granddaughter Emily. I have not returned for a full re-evaluation, which I feel should be done after the first five years, because the insurance feels that as long I see my neurologist, Dr. Stubler, on a regular basis to keep up with any significant progress or changes in my condition that is all they are interested in to follow the stroke.

The recovery road is not an easy one, but it is a necessary path for each and every one to consider when faced with this crisis. I have tried to include some personal history, some education, and a little advice I feel will be helpful to the person suffering a stroke or that is at risk for a stroke. My main goal in this book is that of assistance, for it is a hard fact to face, that you "will need assistance," some a little, some a lot. The previous chapter on prevention is just that. I hope to assist those who may be faced with cardiovascular disease, or other factors related to a possible stroke in the future. I know it may not be you, but the statistics show that one in four will be faced with a CVD-related condition at some time in their health history and nearly 50 percent of those diagnosed with CVD will become heart attack or stroke victims. Don't take the prevention chapter lightly. You can prevent CVD and stroke if you start now and change the lifestyle habits that make you a prime risk candidate for such an unforgettable and life changing event!

My stroke was rather unusual because it was precipitated by a *pheochromocytoma*, a small tumor of the adrenal gland that is lethal, and fatal for many. It was not caused by the typical stroke symptoms but rather by adrenal stress, either 'eustress' or 'distress.' Those of you familiar with the work of Harvard physiologist Walter Cannon or Canada's Hans Selye, on the physiology of stress will understand how 'distress' and 'eustress' work. Those of you that are not familiar still know what distress is but few are familiar with the term eustress. This is where the body is under constant pressure to perform like an outstanding athlete or performer. They love what they are doing and it is not a distress to them mentally or emotionally, but it causes stress to the adrenal gland just the same. I was a workaholic and didn't realize it. The doctors think the relentless work (stress) precipitated my tumor. Even though I loved every phase of my life, I worked tirelessly and did not give my adrenal time to recoup. I was very much like an adrenalin junkie that constantly kept the adrenalin pumping in my work effort. I somehow didn't realize this even after my wife said that I was working too long and hard. I thought of course, she was being overly protective.

Now, as I look back on it, I had worked hard all my life. Growing up as a poor boy from West Virginia drove me to want to better my condition in life. I watched my father work 12-hour shifts in the coalmine and come home and play music or work on building a house for someone on weekends. I just thought hard work went with the territory. I worked all through high school and all through college, sometimes taking double shifts in the food cannery, while I was attending college in Maryland. This often meant two 10- hour shifts seven days a week all summer.

So, I never blinked in graduate school when I taught a 6 AM medical terminology course, then went to class all day and practiced my martial arts from 6 to 8 PM, and then worked as a projectionist at the movie theater from 9 to midnight. Then I would go home and study from 1:00 to3:00 AM and get up and do it all over again four or five days a week. Even after finishing a bachelor's, masters and a chiropractic degree I didn't stop. I went on to complete three other doctoral programs. I guess I just love to work. I would wonder sometimes when people would call me the Energizer Bunny or Dr. Go because I didn't believe my routine was excessive.

The Japanese have a word for it-*karoshi*, or "death by overwork." But, can stress from work really do you in? Finnish researchers decided to find out. The years 1991 to 1993 in Finland were as bad as it generally gets economically, with unemployment nearly tripling to 17 percent. Those who survived the downsizing had to assume greater workloads. During this period and for seven years afterward, Dr. Jussi Vahtera and psychologist Mika Kivimaki at the Finnish Institute of Occupational Health in Helsinki followed municipal workers who survived the cutbacks in four towns. Their sobering conclusion appeared in the 2003 British Medical Journal. Kivimaki put it bluntly: "The only difference in the mortality was in cardiovascular deaths. Those in units which downsized and worked the most suffered twice the death rate from heart attack and stroke."

My father always had a couple of memorable quotes that he would tell me whether I wanted to hear them or not, " if you ever want to get ahead in life you better not be afraid of work" and "a little work never killed anybody." But, I believe in my case that may have been wrong. My stroke brought on by overwork and stress almost killed me. However, I have to admit, my dad said "a little work" and as usual I would always think, well, if a little is good, more is better. It was not the case this time!

Many have asked why a holistic doctor like me did not pick up on the fact that I had something as lethal as an adrenal tumor. I was in the Chiropractic and Acupuncture professions, examined and treated by at least a dozen or more of my colleagues and no one suspected the tumor. For that matter, neither did any of the medical doctors I had seen in the five or so years for physicals and screening tests before the stroke. I was by all standards in "perfect health!"

I would like to mention in this closing chapter that I learned a great deal about stroke while I was doing research for this book. An aspect I was unaware was the connection between Viagra, the sexual performance drug and stroke. Viagra has brought the whole world to 'attention' but it caught my attention for a different reason than most men. It has been hailed as a possible treatment for strokes. Animal studies have shown that Viagra can improve memory and movement by helping damaged brains develop new cells and blood vessels. The Henry Ford Hospital in Detroit has spent 10 years studying stroke recovery with Viagra. Dr. Michael Chopp, head of neurological research, said: "What we found is that we can use drugs like Viagra to create new brain cells. Those that are treated do much better. There are far fewer functional deficits. Days later there is reduced neurological deficit and new brain cells."

Now the researchers are planning to recruit human patients between ages 18 and 80 for the next phase of their research. I have sent in my application!

I recently finished a book sent to me by Mariah, my daughter, called *"Peeling the Onion: Reversing the Ravages of*

Stroke" by Robin Robinson. This book introduces a new theory of medical treatment for stroke, the introduction of a great deal of medication (vasodilators) into the body to open up the blood flow in the damaged blood vessels. I agree with this hypothesis by William Hammesfahr, MD, because this is one of the aims of acupuncture treatment. Dr. Hammesfahr states that you must remain on these medications for the rest of your life or the symptoms will return.

However, despite the vasodilatation treatment, I don't agree with the philosophy because it is still "treatment" oriented instead of "prevention" directed. I feel prevention of the stroke and CVD should be the key thrust behind an effective program, and then if the prevention doesn't work for some reason, institute the medical treatment program. Research dollars then can be spent on those few people that will not follow the prevention plan and it will be necessary to find out why the blood vessels won't remain open for the life sustaining blood flow. That small percentage may need the medical vasodilators as a treatment after a stroke incident but the percentage of stroke and CVD would be very small as compared to what the percentage is now.

I have listed some references cited in the back of this book. I'm sure I may have missed some; if I did, I express my regret. I have included a partial reading list of some other important related material everyone should at least be aware of at this time.

In conclusion, I want people to understand a person can be considered "healthy" by modern medicine and still suffer the effects of some of these silent killers like stroke. Again, this is another reason for the emphasis on preventive health care. I cannot say enough about how important this subject is today. The world is faced with a cardiovascular disease epidemic and it must be halted. I want this book to help contribute to that end.

Disclaimer

This book is a trip through the emotions and struggle of one man and that of his caregiver. It is not a medical prescription for individuals, as the process of evaluating patients is very individualized and needs to be done in a controlled medical environment. This story is creative non-fiction. It is seen through the author's eyes and memory rebounding from the stroke. While some of the names are correct, the names of the patients and other medical personnel have been changed. Any inaccuracies in the book are entirely mine and do not reflect on the medical community.

John L. Stump, 2007 (first printing)
John L. Stump, 2018 (second printing)

Dr. John L. Stump

Reading Group Questions

I. Was this book presented in layman's definitions and terms that were not too difficult for the reader to understand?
II. Was the reader able to easily follow the progression of the author with his stroke story?
III. Was this a creative nonfiction account able to justify the brevity of such a devastating disease?

Book Summary

This unusual and amazing story unfolds the night after the author returns home from doing an acupuncture lecture in Richmond, Virginia. Goes to dinner with his wife then returns home where they begin packing for and up-coming Sports medicine lecture trip to New Zealand. While packing, Doc reports that he began to have an unusual feeling in his right arm when trying to get his wife, Dianne's attention, he could not talk. He looked up at the clock and the time was nearly midnight. Three weeks later he woke up in the hospital the victim of a massive stroke.

This story tells the feeling and struggle Dr. John Stump and his wife Dianne, experienced after the sudden and unexpected cardiovascular incident that one-third of the American adults are subject to having after the age of fifty. The later chapters of the book, also provides the reader with the essential knowledge one needs to help from becoming a future stroke victim. Many useful names and addresses are used in the reference section as well as, a reading group outline of questions that may be used for a discussion group.

Discussion Points

1. What is a stroke? Where does it occur?

2. Are there different types of strokes? What are they?

3. Do strokes only happen to old people?

4. Is stroke age, gender or race specific?

5. What are the signs of a stroke?

6. What is a TIA?

7. Is a pheochromocytoma a common cause of a stroke?

8. Can strokes be prevented? How?

9. What lifestyles changes would be the most important to make for stroke prevention?

10. Would you know the signs and symptoms of stroke now?

Author Questions and Answers

1. What was the purpose of writing the Stroke of Midnight?

    My initial purpose for writing this book was to get the message out to the public that a stroke is preventable in most cases. I didn't want others going through what I have had to deal with from this stroke incident.

2. Why present the book in narrative form?

    I wanted to tell my story because I was the most unlikely candidate for a stroke that you could possibly think. I wanted to have people know a doctor's struggle process from the initial incident through the recovery was the same as it was for everyone that have the misfortune of a stroke.

3. Why was there stroke information in each chapter instead of one chapter with all the information concerning stroke?

    I felt the reader could learn and retain much more of the story and the stroke information if it was presented in this form. As a result you will find each chapter contains some good information, some a little more some less.

4. Why is there one chapter with a heavy emphasis on prevention?

    It was my intention to have the reader understand they have a choice about getting the conditions that cause a stroke. They also needed to understand how to implement this lifestyle change if they knew they had signs and wanted to prevent a stroke.

5. Why was the author's stroke different from most other strokes?

Most strokes come from a cardiovascular compromise. The author's stroke came from an adrenal tumor called a pheochromocytoma. This type of tumor is very lethal and few have the good results of recovery and rehabilitation of the author.

A STROKE OF MIDNIGHT…

The Numbers You Should Know To Help Manage Your Heart Health

Diagnostic & Monitoring Test

Electrocardiogram (ECG or EKG) activity and heartbeat	Gives a prompt view of the heart's electrical rhythm	Note: The first three procedures in this chart reflect the generally accepted screening recommendations from national health organizations and experts.
Exercise EKG Test	Monitors the electrical activity of the heart while exercising, which stresses the heart by increasing the need for oxygen	
Cardiac catheterization	Uses a catheter to trace blood flow back to the heart. Checks for blockages and narrowing in the coronary arteries that supply blood to the heart muscle	
Echocardiogram (ECHO)	Uses ultrasound to elevate heart chamber size, heart valve function, and how well the heart is pumping blood	

Dr. John L. Stump

Diagnostic & Monitoring Test

PROCEDURE	WHEN OR WHY	OPTIMAL LEVELS
Screening Test		
Fasting cholesterol panel	Beginning at age 25, then every five years if it is borderline or elevated	Total: 199 or lower HDL: 60 or higher LDL: 99 or lower Triglycerides: <149
Blood Pressure check	Beginning at age 21, at each doctor visit, or at least once every two years	Normal: <120/80 Prehypertension: < 139/89 Hypertension: > 140/90
Fasting plasma glucose (tests for diabetes)	Beginning at age 40, or earlier and more often with risk factors	Normal: <100 mg/dl Prediabetes: 101-125 Diabetes: >126 mg/dl

Reference Sources

Acubriefs Newsletter 4th Quarter Winter 2004 www.acubriefs

Acupuncture for Stroke, On the Horizon. Prevention page 164, February 2003

Albert, C. M., et al. "Blood levels of long-chain n-3 fatty acids and the risk of sudden death." New England Journal of Medicine 346 (2002): 1113–1118.

American Heart Association. Heart and Stroke Statistical Update. Dallas, TX: AHA, 2002.

Awareness Campaign for Women about Heart Disease. National Heart, Lung and Blood Institute (NHLBI) http://www.nhlbi.nih.gov/health/hearttruth/index.htm

AARP Bulletin. Is the Stroke Belt Moving? Health, May 2005.

Benson, H., Corliss, J. and Cowley, G. "Brain Check" Newsweek, September 27, 2004

Burkman, K. "The Stroke Recovery Book"

Centers for Disease Control and Prevention. Disparities in deaths from stroke among persons aged <75 years - United States, 2002. MMWR Morb Mortal Wkly Rep. 2005; 54:477-481.

Campbell, T.C. The China Study. Benbella Books, Dallas, TX 2004.

D'Admao, Peter J. Eat Right For Your Type. G.P. Putnam's Sons, New York, 1996.

Davis, B. Oriental Medicine Taijiquan Journal, Minnesota College of Acupuncture and Oriental Medicine, 2001.

Douglass, William C. "Avoiding Heart Disease May Be Easier Than You Think" www.HSIResearch, September 02, 2004.

Electroacupuncture: A Practical Manual and Resource, Elsevier Ltd, London NW1 7 BY, March, 2006 – Edited by David Mayor.

Goldberg B Heart Disease & High Blood Pressure. Tiburon, CA: Future Medicine Publishing, 1998.

Goodnight, S. H., et al. "Assessment of the therapeutic use of n-3 fatty acids in vascular disease and thrombosis." Chest 102, no. 4 Suppl. (1992): 374S–384S.

Hachinski, V. & Hachinski, L. Stroke: A Comprehensive Guide to Brain Attacks. Richmond Hill, ON, Canada: Firefly Books, 2001.

Journal of the American Chiropractic Association, For Your Health "Stroke: Known What to Do," August 2004.

Journal of American Geriatric Society, 2006 Exercise May Reduce Depressive Symptoms After Stroke, 54: 240-247.

Kent C. Stress, Distress, and Vertebral Subluxation, Research on Purpose, The Chiropractic Journal, December 2004.

Kinsella, J. E., et al. "Dietary n-3 polyunsaturated fatty acids and amelioration of cardiovascular disease: Possible mechanisms." American Journal of Clinical Nutrition 52, no. 1 (1990): 1–28.

Martin T. Smoking Cessation. After the last cigarette. http://quitsmoking.aboutcom/cs/afterquitting/a after quitting.htm

McLeod N, Stroke Prevention: Know Your Risk, Manage Your Risk, Healthy Living, Thomas Hospital, August, 2005.

Medline Plus, Medical Encyclopedia: Pheochromocytoma, 2004 www.nlm.nih.gov

Morris D, Buettner T, White E, Aquatic Community-Based Exercise Programs For Stroke Survivors, The Journal of Physical Therapy, Vol. 4 No. 2, August 1996.

Olajide Williams, MD, Assistant Professor of Neurology, Columbia University, New York, NY; Director, Harlem Hospital Stroke Initiative, New York, NY, Email: owilliams@neuro.columbia.edu

Rath, Matthias. Cancer. Santa Clara, CA: M/R Publishing, 2001.

Reuters Medical News, Possible New Indication for Viagra: Stroke 2002 www.medscape.com

Sacco RL, Boden-Albala B, Abel G, et al. Race-ethnic disparities in the impact of stroke risk factors: the Northern Manhattan Stroke Study. 2001; 32:1725-1731.

Santos, Daniel. Feng Shui for the Body: Balancing Body and Mind for a Healthier Life. Wheaton, IL: Quest Books, 1998.

Selye H "The Stress of Life," New York, McGraw Hill, Co. 1984.

Starwynn, D "Microcurrent Acupuncture" Desert Heart Press, Phoenix, 2002

Stroh, S. and I. Elmadfa. "Invitro studies of the effect of different mixture proportions of omega- 3 and omega-6 fatty acids on thrombocyte aggregation and thromboxane synthesis in human thrombocytes." Zeitung Ernahrungswiss 30, no. 3 (1991): 192–200.

Sun Online Reporter, "Viagra Cure For Strokes" www.thesun.co.uk, February 2005.

The Journal of Nutrition 'Multivitamins May Reduce Heart Attack Risk" 133: 2650-2654, 2003.

The New Medicine Show, by the Editors of Consumer Reports Books, Consumers Union, New York, 1989.

Underwood, A "For a Happy Heart" Newsweek, September 27, 2004.

Voelker R, No Small Concern, The Rotarian, September 2005.

Watkins e'th: Watkins AL, "A Manual of Electrotherapy" Henry Kimpton, London 1968.

Yam D., et al. "The effect of omega-3 fatty acids on risk factors for cardiovascular diseases." Harefuah 140, no. 12 (2001): 1156–1158.

Yau PS Scalp Needling Therapy Medicine & Health Publishing Co. Hong Kong, 1975

Selected Reading and helpful information

Stroke...Your Complete Exercise Guide by Gordon N.

Is acupuncture effective in stroke rehabilitation? by Tang JL and Zhan SY, jltang@cuhk.edu.hk

Therapeutic efficiency of laser and Electroacupuncture in cerebral circulation insufficiency by Nikolaev NA

Real Men See Doctors, Your Health, AARP Bulletin February 2004

Acupuncture in Stroke Treatment by Erickson R, American Academy of Medical Acupuncture, August 2004 www.medicalacupuncture.org

Heart Disease, Stroke & High Blood Pressure by Goldberg B and the Editors of Alternative Medicine Digest

American Heart Association http://www.aha.org

American College of Cardiology http://www.acc.org

Cleveland Clinic Heart Center, Understanding Coronary Artery Disease. http://www.cevelandclinic.org/heartcenter/pub/guide/disease/cad/understandingcad.htm

American Acupuncture Association – www.aaom.org

American Chiropractic Association – www.americanchiropracticassociation.org

American Naturopathic Association – www.naturopathic.org

Medical Laser Systems – www.medicallasersystems.com

Nutritional Associations – www.healthplusweb.com

Standard Process Company – www.standardprocess.com

Trace Mineral Analysis Company – www.tracemineralanalysis.com

Rotary International - http://www.rotary.org

Laser Organizations – www.lasernu.org

National Cholesterol Education Program. National Heart, Lung, and Blood Institute (NHLBI) http://www.nhlbi.nih.gov/about/ncep/

Acupuncture Today – www.acupuncturetoday.com

About The Author

John L. Stump, DC, OMD, PhD, EdD, has a varied and colorful academic background. As an athlete, he became interested in the function of the human body. After he received his undergraduate degree at the University of Maryland, he taught high school biology for several years before an auto accident temporarily altered his teaching and coaching career. After the accident, he decided to attend graduate school full time where he became interested in natural health. After graduate school, he decided on medical school but leaned toward natural health and prevention and graduated the "most out-standing graduate" from Palmer College of Chiropractic in Davenport, Iowa. In 1976, while obtaining his doctorate degree, he met a Japanese doctor who introduced him to the ancient practice of Acupuncture and the Zen Buddhist art of Shorinji Kempo. He then went on to pursue post-doctoral training in acupuncture in Japan and China, which led to his degrees in Acupuncture (OMD) and Oriental Medicine (PhD) as well as a fifth degree Black Belt in Shorinji Kempo.

Shortly after he returned from the Orient he was asked to head a team of doctors for the 1986 Asian Games and the 1988 Seoul Olympics. This turned his interest toward Sports Medicine and ended with the doctorate in Education being awarded by the United States Sports Academy. Dr. Stump went on to become an internationally known lecturer and expert in the field of natural health care with specialties in chiropractic, manipulation (Tunia), acupuncture and nutrition. He has written several books in those fields and is a contributing author on several other textbooks. This is his first creative solo writing adventure out of the pure academic area.

He is an active member of Rotary International and has a special interest in health care and cardiovascular disease eradication. He is also a member of numerous professional and research organizations. Dr. Stump is married to Dianne Bearden and they have three children, Mariah, Mike and Chad. Dr. Stump is now happy to be called "Pop-Pau" when his children and their children come to visit.

After returning home from a lecture in Richmond, Virginia in May 1999, he was suddenly struck down by a stroke at 53 years of age. Three weeks later he awoke to realize his whole life had changed.

This is the story of how a health professional dealt with this devastating event and his struggle back to a fulfilled and happy life.

Dr. Stump may be contacted at Doc@DocStump.com.